COMMERCIAL LIGHTING

creating dynamic public spaces

D1027858

ROCKPORT
PUBLISHERS

Rockport Publishers, Inc.
Gloucester, Massachusetts
Distributed by North Light Books,
Cincinnati, Ohio

First published in the United States of America by:
Rockport Publishers, Inc.
33 Commercial Street
Gloucester, Massachusetts 01930-5089
Telephone: (508) 282-9590
Fax: (508) 283-2742

Distributed to the book trade and the art tradein the
United States by:
North Light, an imprint of
F&W Publications
1507 Dana Avenue
Cincinnati, Ohio 45207
Telephone: (513) 531-2222

Other Distribution by:
Rockport Publishers
Gloucester, Massachusetts 01930

ISBN 1-56496-440-X

10 9 8 7 6 5 4 3 2 1

Art Director: Laura P. Herrmann
Designer: Minnie Cho Design

Front Cover Photograph: Le Bonheur Children's Medical Center
                    credit on page 141

Back Cover Photographs: (top) Urban Eyes Optometry Boutique #1
                    credit on page 8
                    (bottom) Gunne Sax Clothing Corporate Offices
                    credit on page 136

Manufactured in China

DEDICATION

I would like to dedicate this book to

all the creative, wonderful people

whose lives have been cut short by AIDS.

They were our friends, our family members,

and our lovers. We miss them terribly.

ACKNOWLEDGEMENTS

It takes a huge number of people to put a book like this

together. I would like to thank all the designers and architects

who contributed their fine work, along with the photographers

who so skillfully captured the magic of these projects.

I want to give my sincere appreciation to Tim Brace, Rodel Rosel,

and Takae Oyake, without whose help this book would not have

come together. I'm also grateful to Catherine Ng for keeping

the business afloat while I was mentally drowning.

FOREWORD

Historically, there have been one or two things wrong with most books about lighting design. Either they are written by engineers and illustrated with abstract line drawings and poorly reproduced black-and-white photographs of mundane, out-of-date projects, or they are colorful, coffee-table books written by non-designers who haven't got a clue about how lighting works or what the photographs are meant to show. The author of this book, Randall Whitehead, is not only an able writer, but a highly qualified lighting designer as well. With these unique abilities, he has produced a book that finally bridges the gap: It is both instructive and beautiful.

Those of us who study the history of buildings from a lighting perspective know that the stories of many of our most familiar buildings have gone untold because they have gone unrecorded. For just this reason, COMMERCIAL LIGHTING is bound to have a place in libraries for many, many years. In the near future, it will be studied by lighting designers seeking information and inspiration. In the distant future, it will be a valuable document for those who study historic lighting. Some will examine it to learn the stories behind the lighting; others will look at it with an eye toward restoring the original lighting systems in these buildings. As a historical record, COMMERCIAL LIGHTING will become an indispensable resource.

Charles D. Linn, AIA
Managing Senior Editor
Architectural Record
New York City

COMMERCIAL LIGHTING DESIGN: CREATING DYNAMIC PUBLIC SPACES

Lighting design can make or break a project. Although it is often the last aspect of construction to be considered, and the first to get trimmed from the budget, well-designed lighting is critical to the success of commercial interiors. Good lighting draws attention to projects and puts customers at ease; bad lighting glares, drawing attention to itself and away from the merchandise.

Today, advances in lighting design technology are solving old problems and offering many new options for commercial spaces. In the last few years, the two standard choices—fluorescent and incandescent lights—have been joined by a host of high-intensity discharge (H.I.D.) lights, and all three types have undergone tremendous refinements in what they can do, and how well they do it.

In commercial spaces, lighting serves three primary functions:

Accent Lighting

Accent illumination highlights objects (everything from merchandise and art to mannequins and plants). If displays change frequently, the accent light needs to be highly flexible; halogen bridge systems, track lighting, or recessed adjustable fixtures are all good choices. Also, choosing fixtures that are shielded and can accommodate a louver will cut glare and keep the focus on the highlighted object.

Task Lighting

Task lights illuminate work and work areas; desk lamps, the under-shelf fixture at a work station, and vanity fixtures in dressing rooms are all task lights. The optimum position for task lighting is between the user's head and the work surface. If an area is lit from directly above, users end up working in their own shadows.

Ambient Lighting

Ambient light fills the volume of space with a glow of illumination. It softens shadows, makes people look better, and makes environments more inviting. The best ambient light is light that is bounced off the ceiling. Wall sconces, torchieres, cove lighting, and pendant-hung fixtures are all good sources of ambient light.

All of these functions are covered throughout the text, along with the latest advances in fluorescent, incandescent, mercury vapor, high-pressure sodium, and metal halide lighting.

A visual feast of commercial projects from around the world, this book demonstrates how light can be incorporated into commercial designs in visually stunning ways.

Shedding some new light on commercial applications

Advancements in lamp technology are offering many new techniques—and refinements on some old ones—for lighting commercial spaces.

If you've been around lighting at all, you know that a **lamp** in this industry is a **light bulb** to everyone else. What you may not know is how far lamps have come in the last few years and what that can mean to lighting a commercial space.

Fluorescents

The biggest change in fluorescents is the variety of colors now available. For 30 years, the choice was cool white or warm white. Cool white gave everything a greenish cast, while warm white put out an orange/pink light that was supposed to match incandescent, but didn't. There are now more than 200 colors available in fluorescent lamps.

The color of lamps is measured in **degrees of Kelvin**. The lower the degrees Kelvin, the more orange the light; the higher the degrees Kelvin, the bluer the light. At one end of the normal spectrum is incandescent light, rated at 2,800 degrees Kelvin; at the other end is cool white at 5,000 degrees Kelvin. Staying within the 3,000 to 4,000 degrees Kelvin range produces good **color rendition** (which is less faithful to how color looks in sunlight, but more complimentary to skin tones). The key to success is in balancing good illumination with a "human" quality of light.

Daylight or **full-spectrum** fluorescent lamps offer a good approximation of daylight. Since colors are truest in daylight, these lamps are excellent for color-matching applications (clothing stores, art stores, etc.) Cooler color temperatures don't do much for skin appearance, though, because they are in the unflattering 5000-6250 degrees Kelvin range. A compromise at 3500-4000 degrees Kelvin is better for commercial work. Remember, in a public setting like a hotel, restaurant, or clothing store, lighting the people is just as important as lighting the space.

Incandescents

The focus of much of the innovation in incandescent sources of light has been low-voltage lamps (nothing beats low voltage for controlled beam spreads). A simple vase can become a dazzling jewel when lit with a 50-watt, **MR16EXT** (multi-mirror reflector spot) or a 50-watt, **PAR 36 NSP** (parabolic reflector narrow spot). Because of the relationship of the lamp to the integral reflector, these 50-watt lamps can produce a bright concentration of illumination.

Another advantage of low voltage is the compact size of the lamps, allowing for much smaller fixtures both in track and recessed versions. The MR16 lamp is two inches by two inches, yet it offers nearly the same amount of punch as a 150-watt, 150R40SP reflector lamp, which is five inches by seven inches. The fixtures themselves are often barely larger than the lamps.

A drawback to using low-voltage systems in a commercial installation is the relatively short life of the lamps. They are rated anywhere from 300 to 3,500 hours (depending on the beam spread and the manufacturer), making maintenance costs a major factor.

Another factor is that low-voltage systems require transformers. Electricians are usually most comfortable with **integral transformer** systems, because all of the wiring up to the fixture is standard line-voltage. This setup creates a higher initial cost, since each unit must have its own transformer. Also, transformers emit a "hum"; the more transformers, the louder the humming sound. Although the humming noise won't be an important consideration in high-traffic areas, such as hallways, it should be taken into account in lighting plans for quiet areas, such as work stations, or libraries.

Transformer remote systems run one or more fixtures from a single transformer, cutting down considerably on material costs. However, as they may lower wattage consumption they increase amperage, which requires careful use of the correct gauge wire.

Voltage drop is another important consideration. Some fixtures in a "run" may—if they are more than 100 feet away from the transformer—put out less light than those closer to the transformer. A centrally located transformer, or group of transformers, helps correct the problem.

H.I.D. [High Intensity Discharge]

H.I.D. is coming into its own in interior commercial applications. Supermarkets are now using H.I.D. lamps, and other retail businesses won't be far behind. These lamps are the most energy-efficient on the market and have the highest lumen output. There are four discharge technologies:

Mercury vapor lamps produce a blue-white light that has typically been used in street lamps. It has poor color-rendering properties on the whole, but it does make green plants come alive. As a result, mercury vapor lamps are often used around landscaping.

High-pressure sodium lamps cast a yellow-orange light. They are most commonly spotted in major roadway lighting (replacing mercury vapor), at baked goods displays in grocery stores, and lighting brick. The Golden Gate Bridge is illuminated with high-pressure sodium lamps.

Low-pressure sodium lamps produce an orange-gray light that makes most everything look the same color. Often used for roadways and parking lot lighting, thanks to their long life and great lumen output. These lamps render color so poorly that ambulance crews at accident sites lit with low-pressure sodium lamps complain that they can't tell the difference between water, oil, and blood.

Metal halide lamps are the newest kid on the block. They have the best color-rendering qualities of all the H.I.D. sources and come in color temperatures of three, four, and five thousand degrees Kelvin. Metal halide is being used more and more as a source of indirect ambient light for airports, hotel lobbies and retail spaces.

Be aware that H.I.D. lamps can shift in color at approximately halfway through their rated life. Some shift to green, and some to magenta, and the shift is not always consistent from lamp to lamp, or from manufacturer to manufacturer.

Fluorescents have a similar problem. At about 11,000 hours into their 22,000-hour rated lamp life, they can produce up to twenty percent less light than when they were new, while still using the same amount of power. Currently, the best way to beat this problem is to anticipate it and replace the lamps before the halfway point.

Dimming Controls

Though not they are not lamps themselves, switching and dimming controls are an important part of many lighting designs because of the control they bring to the rest of the system. Dimming has obvious advantages, but also poses certain challenges with various light sources.

Dimming regular incandescent lamps will help extend their life, but it will also make their light more yellow the further they are dimmed. **Quartz** (tungsten halogen) lamps produce a whiter light (3,000 degrees Kelvin) than regular incandescents, but even this becomes amber when dimmed.

There's also another potential problem with dimming quartz. Within each lamp is an amount of iodine. When operated at full capacity, the iodine vaporizes and cleans out the inside of the lamp. If the lamp is constantly dimmed, the iodine does not vaporize, and the lamp blackens and may burn out prematurely. However, burning the lamps at capacity just 20 percent of the time will correct this problem.

The best part about dimming fluorescents is that they won't vary dramatically in color, as the dimmed incandescents will. However, until recently, it meant other drawbacks—such as humming ballasts, lamps that flickered when dimmed more than 80 percent, and only being able to dim lamps that were the same length. Newer systems, using solid-state dimming ballasts, will now permit 90 percent to full-range dimming with no hum and no flicker. Costs run about twice as much as those for a standard magnetic dimming system, but, considering the advantages, it's worth a look.

If dimming is just too expensive for the project, there are a couple of techniques that you can use in grouping switches.

The first is to switch only half of the lamps in each fixture, so that 50 percent of the lights can be kept off during daylight hours, and the remaining lights turned on in the evening.

The second method is to put fixtures that are closest to the windows on separate switches, so that they can be turned off when the sun is shining in. Photo and motion sensors are also products that can control usage and energy costs.

Throughout the text, you'll find examples of these lighting techniques, and many more, all from design professionals working together to develop cohesive, creative results.

chapter one

Well-designed lighting for a retail store is crucial. A customer's willingness to come in and make a purchase is greatly influenced by their comfort level and their reaction to what they see. A drab, dark, or too-brightly lit store can distract customers from the retailer's main focus—the merchandise.

The entrance of a store should welcome customers and invite them inside. Low-level lighting is a poor choice, since most people have an instinctive aversion to going into dark places: low illumination may make customers feel they are entering a cave. Stores can be overly bright, too. People do not like to be blasted by light, they just want to be invited in. A well-designed lighting plan avoids both extremes by incorporating enough ambient light. Ambient, or fill light, reflecting from walls and ceilings, makes spaces seem larger, and helps all areas of a shop come clearly into view.

Too often, stores put accent light on the merchandise, but neglect overall lighting for the patrons. A lighting design that flatters the customers as much as it does the product works to build sales. Clothing stores in particular have found that if the lighting makes the customers look good, they tend to buy more clothes. Similar to the lighting approach recommended for restaurants, ambient light combined with some task and accent lighting is the most successful plan for retail environments. Unlike restaurant lighting, however, retail lighting must maintain a difficult balance between offering flattering light and light that approximates daylight enough for matching colors.

The projects in this chapter demonstrate innovative approaches to striking this balance while creating lush, exciting spaces.

DR. ALBERT C. LEE
HOURS
MON. - FRI. 11-8
SATURDAY 9-6
SUNDAY 12-5

URBAN EYES

project   **Urban Eyes Optometry**
           Boutique #1
           San Francisco, CA
lighting   **John Lum Architecture**
architect   **John Lum Architecture**
interior   **John Lum Architecture**
photographer   **Sharon Risedorph**

A flexible, track lighting system mounted above the ceiling line projects a vibrant halogen light to illuminate the structural column. The surface patina is textured with the impressions of the optometric instruments, antique eyewear, and the architect's and optometrist's handprints.

project   **Urban Eyes   Optometry**
           Boutique #1
lighting   **John Lum Architecture**
architect   **John Lum Architecture**
interior   **John Lum Architecture**
photographer   **Sharon Risedorph**

Back lighting eyewear is a relatively new concept. Many of today's frames have a translucent quality that shows best when illuminated from behind. Color-corrected fluorescents double as task lights in the storage area located directly behind the Shoji-like display. Simple, dynamic pendant fixtures project light through a hole in the top of these free-standing displays. Single frames get a jewelry store treatment.

Urban Eyes Optometry Boutique San Francisco California

If ever a shop could dispel the myth that glasses are unappealing, it is the Urban Eyes installation on an upscale part of Market Street. The shop's 1,000-square foot interior by John Lum of John Lum Architecture proclaims a decidedly hip and sophisticated atmosphere, sending the subliminal message that customers who sport this eyewear will be equally urbane.

Working closely with lighting designer Randall Whitehead, the architect laid out the space to accommodate product displays and a dispensing area in front, with the more private functions, such as examination room, lab, and offices, in the back. The public front is designed to play with vision and perspective through manipulation of forms, as well as to present a lively exploration of materials and designed objects that will attract passersby into the store.

Inside, one half of the shop is devoted to the display of glasses and the other to dispensing them. For the fun of clients trying on glasses, the atmosphere is similar to that of a modeling runway. Overall lighting comes from recessed fluorescent fixtures, creating the even, glare-free illumination necessary for a retail establishment that is also an optometric health-care practice. Throughout the store, designers kept the light sources as unobtrusive as possible, so that interior elements could be highlighted without extraneous decoration. All of this is accomplished within the tight confines of California's energy-code restrictions.

The sales area is organized along a sinuous wood deck, with eyewear placed between a series of truncated piers—a metaphorical reference to city buildings as well as a practical response to existing columns. Glass shelves between the piers are cleverly illuminated by well lights, eliminating the need for the glare-producing backlit panels typically found in optometric practices. Between each uplight, PL fluorescent fixtures glow behind etched mirrors to create a flattering light. This section is further defined by a wheelchair-accessible wood deck, uplit by well lights.

A perforated metal wall provides additional eyeglass display through the use of removable ribbed plastic shelves. Low-voltage track fixtures mounted on top of the screen highlight the stylized graffiti behind, while recessed MR16 spots add sparkle to the eyeglasses on the adjustable shelves.

Sequestered under the mezzanine stairs is a Buddha shrine and small fish aquarium, elements regarded important to the well being of the store. These niches are illuminated by recessed incandescent "A" lamps, creating a hidden glow that intrigues the customers. The random steel-rod banister expresses a frenetic energy that contrasts with the meditative calmness of the staircase.

project **Urban Eyes Optometry Boutique #1 San Francisco, CA**

lighting **John Lum Architecture**

architect **John Lum Architecture**

interior **John Lum Architecture**

photographer **Sharon Risedorph**

Because of the very small square footage of Urban Eyes' first store, the architect employed lighting as a way of making the space seem larger. Creating vignettes within the areas of light and dark visually expands the surroundings. A flexible, miniature track light system highlights the eyewear while producing a cross-hatched shadow effect. These dramatic contrasts produce an intimate atmosphere in keeping with the individualized attention each customer receives in this exclusive boutique.

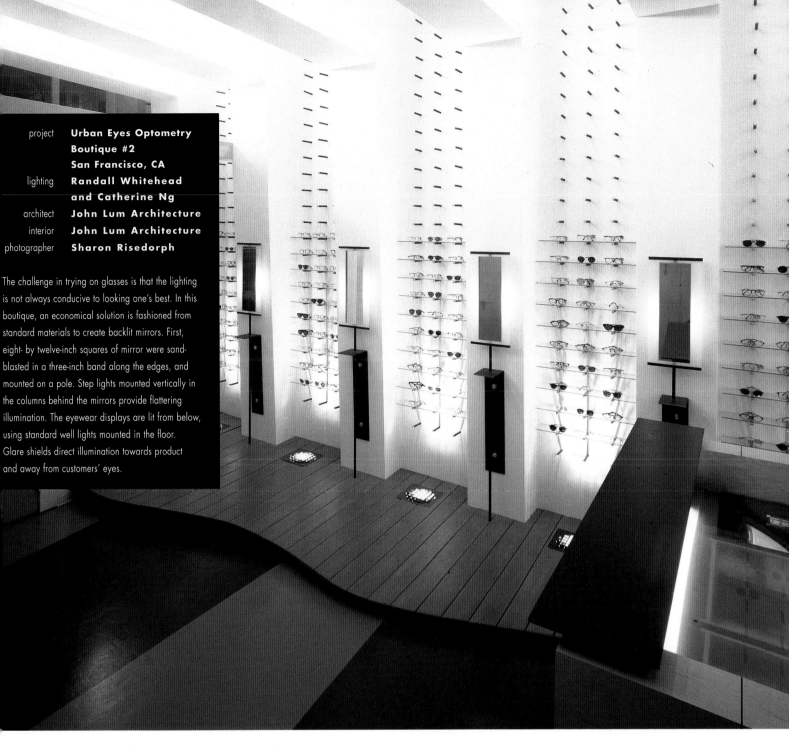

project	**Urban Eyes Optometry Boutique #2 San Francisco, CA**
lighting	**Randall Whitehead and Catherine Ng**
architect	**John Lum Architecture**
interior	**John Lum Architecture**
photographer	**Sharon Risedorph**

The challenge in trying on glasses is that the lighting is not always conducive to looking one's best. In this boutique, an economical solution is fashioned from standard materials to create backlit mirrors. First, eight- by twelve-inch squares of mirror were sand-blasted in a three-inch band along the edges, and mounted on a pole. Step lights mounted vertically in the columns behind the mirrors provide flattering illumination. The eyewear displays are lit from below, using standard well lights mounted in the floor. Glare shields direct illumination towards product and away from customers' eyes.

r e t a i l

project	**Urban Eyes Optometry Boutique #1 San Francisco, CA**
lighting	**John Lum Architecture**
architect	**John Lum Architecture**
interior	**John Lum Architecture**
photographer	**Sharon Risedorph**

A close-up view of shadow play and progressive eyewear treatment.

retail

project	**Confetti Chocolat**
	San Francisco, CA
lighting	**Alan and Joy Ohashi**
architect	**Ohashi Design Studio**
interior	**Ohashi Design Studio**
photographer	**Russell Abraham**

Confetti Chocolat is a highly successful retail store combining gourmet coffee and candy sales in a festive environment with an Italian flavor. This was achieved by separating coffee sales (at left) from chocolate candy sales (center), and carefully studying the layout of coffee equipment so that the queuing up for morning or lunch time coffee did not interfere with the more leisurely browsing for candy. The lighting was designed to be high key, focusing spots, floods, and wall washers on only the merchandise or serving counters to create highlights and shadows for a lively retail environment.

project
The Peppercorn
Carmel, CA

lighting
Donald Maxcy

interior
Donald Maxcy

photographer
Ron Starr

At night, lighting identifies the store's merchandise and continues to "sell" after closing hours—taking advantage of foot traffic past the storefront in the early evening.

project
**Kimono Shop
Tokyo, Japan**
lighting
TL Yamagiwa Lab.
interior
Masanori Umeda
photographer
Yoshio Shiratori

[top] The careful composition of panels in the shapes of clouds, lightning, and rain create an evocative, glowing backdrop.

[bottom] The shapes of clouds, the moon, and migratory birds have been clipped out from an aluminum sheet, like a Kabuki set, (one of the traditional entertainments of Japan). Adjustable back-lighting gives the impression of light reflecting off water, shimmering through the openwork. Products displayed on staggered shelves appear to float.

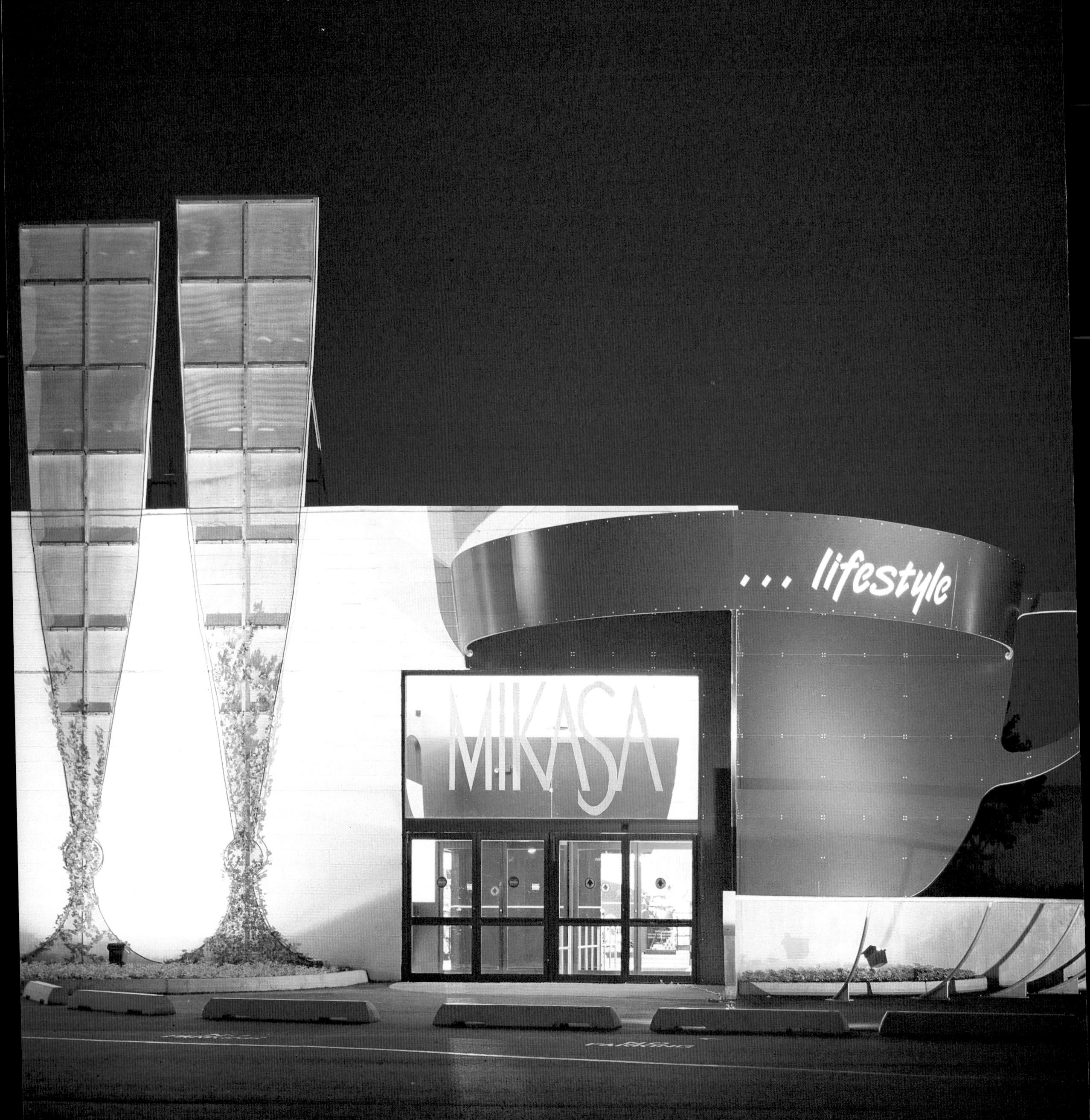

... lifestyle
MIKASA

project
**Mikasa...lifestyle
Secaucus, NJ**
lighting
Paul Haigh
architect
**Haigh Architects
Designers**
interior
**Paul Haigh and
Barbara Haigh**
photographer
Elliot Kaufman

The main entrance is floodlit with exterior-rated halogen fixtures. The entrance vestibule is lit with green-hued fluorescent, while the exit vestibule is lit with red-hued fluorescent.

project	**Mikasa...lifestyle**
	Secaucus, NJ
lighting	**Paul Haigh**
architect	**Haigh Architects Designers**
interior	**Paul Haigh and Barbara Haigh**
photographer	**Elliot Kaufman**

The view of the interior shows the displays and check-out area. An ambient system of industrial fluorescent fixtures positioned to reflect from the underside of the roof deck is balanced by a grid of Par 38 spots on extension wands, aimed to highlight the displayed merchandise.

project
CompUSA
New York, NY
lighting
William Whistler, Brennan Beer
Gorman Monk / Interiors
architect
Sharad Gokarna, Brennan Beer
Gorman Monk / Interiors
interior
William Whistler, Brennan Beer
Gorman Monk / Interiors
photographer
Peter Paige

The curved display wall is lighted with pendant-mounted circular lights, hung flush with the under side of the ceiling grid and painted to match the dark gray structure.

project	**CompUSA**
	New York, NY
lighting	**William Whistler,**
	Brennan Beer Gorman Monk / Interiors
architect	**Sharad Gokarna,**
	Brennan Beer Gorman Monk / Interiors
interior	**William Whistler,**
	Brennan Beer Gorman Monk / Interiors
photographer	**Peter Paige**

The painted sheetrock facia and soffit provide a finished architectural presentation to pedestrians at the retail level, and are complementary to the office tower architecture above. The pale gray reflects light softly, yet creates definition in the retail space.

retail

project
**Smith and Hawken
Stores
Berkeley, CA**

lighting
**Larry French,
S. Leonard Auerbach
& Associates**

architect
Forrest Architects

interior
Forrest Architects

photographer
Douglas A. Salin

The challenge for Smith and Hawken, a gardening and accessories store, was to balance natural light and artificial light in a dynamic way. The warehouse feel of the space was accentuated with surface conduit wiring. Yellow wall-mounted fixtures provide a flexible, easily accessible accent light for displays.

project   **Smith and Hawken Stores
             Berkeley, CA**
lighting   **Larry French, S. Leonard
             Auerbach & Associates**
architect   **Forrest Architects**
interior   **Forrest Architects**
photographer **Douglas A. Salin**

A series of well proportioned pendants, using metal halide lamps, produces a comfortable fill light in a color temperature complementary to the natural light coming in through store windows and skylights. The special ribbed glass adds some sparkle without causing glare.

retail

project **Broadway Market**
Seattle, WA
lighting **Christopher**
Thompson
architect **Cardwell / Thomas**
& Associates Inc.
photographer **David Story**

An intimate shopping atmosphere is created
by diffuse illumination from the skylights, along
with the warm, colorful lighting of the booths
and shops.

retail

project
**Broadway Market
Seattle, WA**

lighting
**Christopher
Thompson**

architect
**Cardwell / Thomas
& Associates Inc.**

photographer
David Story

The curved display wall is
lighted with pendant mounted
circular lights, hung flush with
the under side of the ceiling
grid and painted to match the
dark gray structure.

project
Aurora Superstore
Aurora, CO
lighting
Marty Gregg
architect
Jim Leggit
interior
Bruno Schloffel
photographer
Thomas Arledge

[top] The outdoor gear section is marked by a giant multi-bladed pocketknife, accented with neon and set against a digitally printed topographic map, also highlighted with the occasional neon guideline.

[bottom] A baseball cap with neon "seams" projects from a backdrop of aluminum pennants, identifying the licensed merchandise section.

retail

project
**Z Gallerie
Berkeley, CA**
lighting
**Gensler and
Associates**
interior
**Gensler and
Associates**
photographer
Chas McGrath

Due to budget constraints, the design makes the most of the existing building environment and newly required support systems. Lighting, outlets, electrical conduit, gas lines, sprinklers, HVAC ducts, and diffusers were selected and laid out by the design team. Simple, straightforward display systems such as slatwall and surface mounted brackets are thoughtfully arranged with building systems to create rhythm and pattern, thereby organizing the space. Unobtrusive lighting fixtures bring unique items into focus.

project **Jared, The Galleria of Jewelry Cuyahoga Falls, OH**

lighting **Nicholas P. Zallany**

architect **Nicholas P. Zallany**

interior **Nicholas P. Zallany**

photographer **Jim Maguire**

Inside the main entrance, the torchieres continue to provide decorative as well as practical lighting. The fluorescent showcase lighting puts the jewelry at the center of attention and gives it a glow. Track lighting provides supplementary accent light.

project **Karat Gold North Attleboro, MA**

lighting **Nicholas P. Zalany / Richard R. Jencen Associates**

interior **Nicholas P. Zalany / Richard R. Jencen Associates**

photographer **Alex Beatty**

Peripheral showcases are angled to maximize linear display footage while adding visual interest. Gold jewelry is accentuated with a black background and a combination of daylight, fluorescent, and halogen lighting. The fluorescent lights are hidden inside the floor showcases, while the halogens are suspended low enough to shine closer to the cases. Since showcases along the perimeter of the store did not allow enough room for large fluorescent strips, halogens were used both to brighten these cases and to accent the jewelry.

project
**World Foot Locker
Freehold, NJ**
lighting
**Hillman DiBernardo
& Associates, Inc.**
architect
Norwood Oliver
interior
**Norwood Oliver
Design Associates, Inc.**
photographer
**Peter Paige, Cutter
Smith Photo, Inc.**

[top] For shoppers' convenience, two versions of raised platforms hold circles of day-glo colored acrylic seating; in both cases, the illumination from the downlights creates the illusion that the brightly colored round seats are edge-lit with bands of neon. Suspended at intervals, triangular screens made of cloth filter bright spotlights to cast dappled "sunlight" on merchandise displays.

[bottom] Here, lighting contributes to the "outdoor stadium atmosphere." Metal halide track fixtures, holding 70- and 150-watt lamps, are installed above the dropped circles in the blue painted ceiling. Although metal halide lamps can color shift with age, the distortion goes unnoticed because of the mix of light sources (six kinds in all) installed throughout the space.

retail

21

project
**BULO, Your Next Step
San Francisco, CA**
lighting
Jerome Fuentes Paredes
architect
Jerome Fuentes Paredes
interior
Jerome Fuentes Paredes
photographer
Juliet Stelzmann

[above] Hardwood floors, tinted in earthy tones, mimic a leafy forest floor with sunlight and shadow. A halogen chandelier, designed to resemble a spider's web, enhances the illusion of natural sunlight breaking through the forest canopy.

[right] Halogen lights top custom-designed cases molded in the fashion of trees. To highlight the shoes on display, the lights are wired through the hollow interior of the cast-iron fixtures.

project	**Bullock's**
	Burbank, CA
lighting	**Yann Leroy, Brennan Beer Gorman / Architects**
	Caleb McKenzie, T. Kondos Associates, Inc.
architect	**David W. Beer, Brennan Beer Gorman / Architects**
interior	**David W. Beer, Brennan Beer Gorman / Architects**
photographer	**Steve McLelland**

The facade features polished granite and stucco in shades of brown and beige accented by metallic screens and glass grills in celadon green and bronze colors.
The top of the building is illuminated at night to create a striking nighttime image, creating the impression of a Hollywood stage set.

project	**Japanese Weekend**
	San Francisco, CA
lighting	**Richard Lee Parker**
architect	**Richard Lee Parker**
interior	**Richard Lee Parker**
photographer	**J.D. Peterson**

Low-voltage pendants provide accent illumination. Soft white walls and natural wood trim reflect diffuse light without glare.

r e t a i l

project	**Japanese Weekend**
	San Francisco, CA
lighting	**Richard Lee Parker**
architect	**Richard Lee Parker**
interior	**Richard Lee Parker**
photographer	**J.D. Peterson**

A lightweight metal frame supports and exterior surface of stainless-steel wire mesh, backlit by fluorescent lights. A portable cylinder, capable of installation in various retail spaces, provides an entertaining focus for children while their mothers try on clothes.

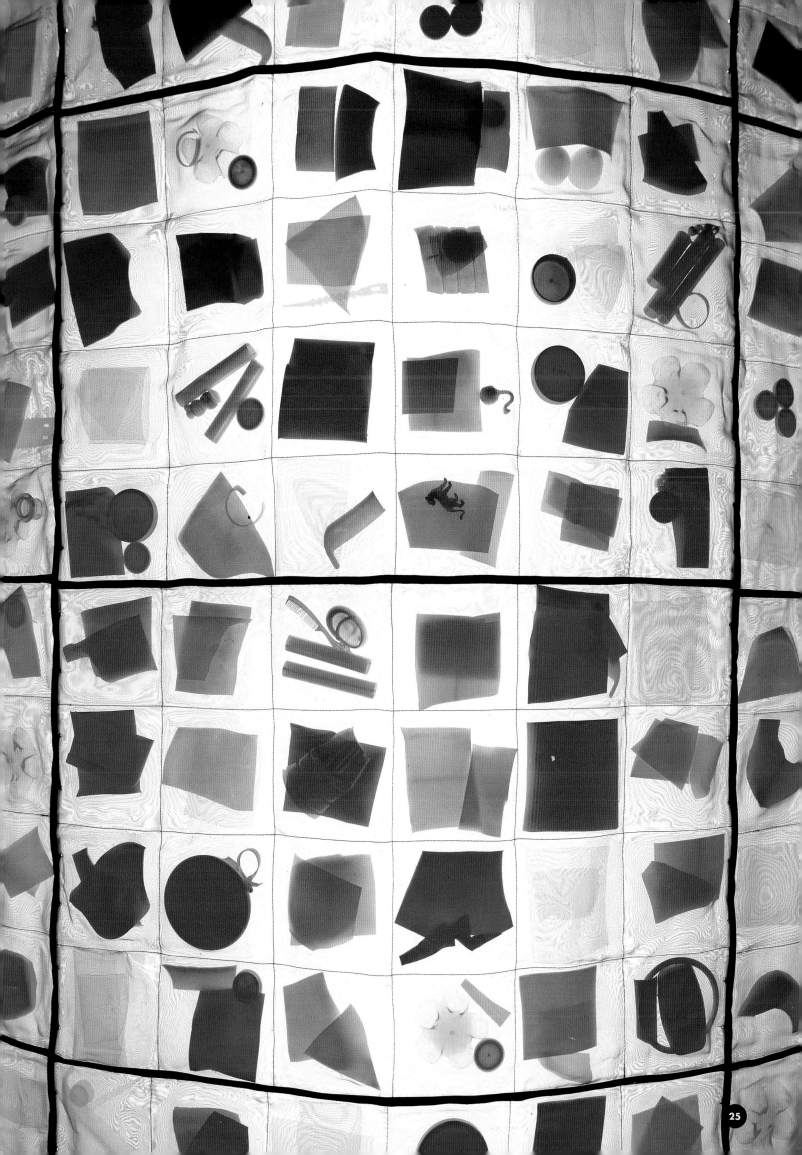

RESTAURANTS

eating well and looking fabulous

A whole new breed of restaurant designers have redefined what it means to go out to dinner. Choices are no longer limited to seats under a hot spotlight, or candlelit alcoves so dark that diners have to fumble for the first course. A wonderful sense of theater has been thrown into the mix, and the result is restaurants that don't sacrifice good lighting for good looks.

Lighting design plays a major role in defining the atmosphere of a restaurant's interior and exterior. Inside, it flatters both the restaurant's design *and* its diners; outside it advertises the restaurant by night with fixtures that don't obscure the building by day.

Ambient light is now getting top billing in most restaurant designs, often coupled with accent lighting to highlight art and greenery.

Designs where each table is illuminated by a spotlight, making diners appear ghoulish the moment they sit down and lean forward, are giving way to those incorporating gentle uplighting from pendant lights, cove lighting, and even votive candles.

The light of track and spot lighting is harsh on faces, it illuminates only the nose, making people's eye sockets seem to recede into blackness.

The effect is similar to holding a flashlight under your chin. The softer effect of ambient lighting takes some planning, especially in restaurants with dark-colored ceilings that don't reflect light well, but is well worth the investment. The ambient effects in the projects that follow demonstrate techniques used by top restaurant designers to flatter both the customers and the cuisine.

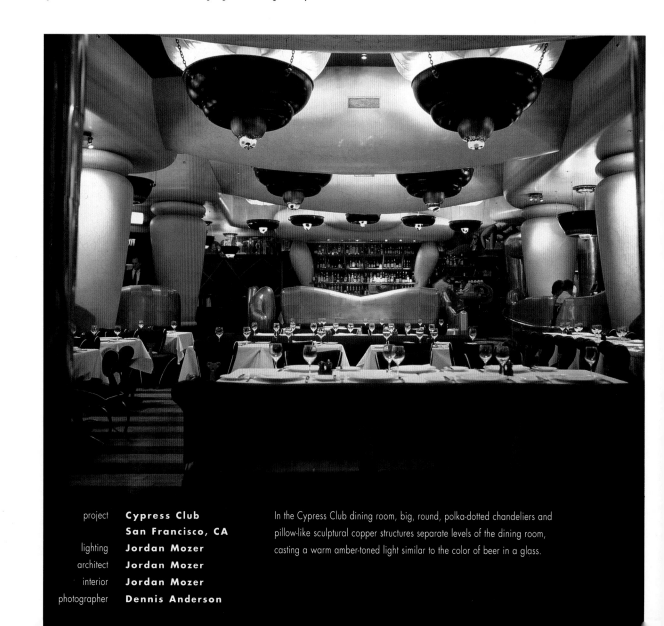

project	**Cypress Club**
	San Francisco, CA
lighting	**Jordan Mozer**
architect	**Jordan Mozer**
interior	**Jordan Mozer**
photographer	**Dennis Anderson**

In the Cypress Club dining room, big, round, polka-dotted chandeliers and pillow-like sculptural copper structures separate levels of the dining room, casting a warm amber-toned light similar to the color of beer in a glass.

project **Cypress Club**
San Francisco, CA
lighting **Jordan Mozer**
architect **Jordan Mozer**
interior **Jordan Mozer**
photographer **Dennis Anderson**

27

project
Cypress Club
San Francisco, CA
lighting
Jordan Mozer
architect
Jordan Mozer
interior
Jordan Mozer
photographer
Dennis Anderson

Sculptural copper "pillows" separate the dining room's two levels. The shape of the dining room chairs were inspired by the fenders of a 1948 "Hudson" car. Lighting is soft and amber in tone, in harmony with the curvy surroundings. The chicken-like sconces on the walls are made of cast bronze and slumped glass, and shaped appropriately for a restaurant resembling a chicken in a prep kitchen more than a one crossing the street.

Cypress Club
San Francisco
California

Jordan Mozer found his inspiration for the Cypress Club in Hollywood's version of San Francisco during the forties. The club's name derives from a fictional restaurant in Raymond Chandler's novel *The Big Sleep*. The design features squat, bigger-than-life columns, ballooning light fixtures, and overstuffed furniture, resulting in a space where Mozer feels "you might find Clark Kent or Roger Rabbit." Curvy forms from 1940s industrial design, such

as the 1948 Hudson car, airplanes, vacuum cleaners, and television sets, decorate the interior, illuminated by the type of soft, indirect lighting favored by fashion photographers.

The entire club is a wild, wonderful indoor fantasy that conjures up images from the whole spectrum of one's imagination; another world down to the last detail, including dishes, furniture, and light fixtures. Maple, mahogany, copper, marble, and stained glass are all part of the look. Diners feel instantly comfortable, with a

slight sense of having been there before.

The lighting design creates a warm, flattering light for romantic dining. Indirect light is the main source of illumination, to avoid any intrusive glare. Lots of uplighting reflects from diffusing materials, including the rich cream, ruby, and amber tones of blown and slumped glass fixtures.

At the center of the room, luminaires have sprinkler heads dropped through their centers. They are positioned to bounce light from the cream-colored velvet drapes

that hang above them (covering electrical drops and speakers in the ceiling.) Fondly referred to as the "Parachuting Donut " lamps, these fixtures are made of blown glass and spun aluminum, as are related fixtures throughout the room.

The perimeter mural is painted in the Depression-era, Work Program style, and is a visual tour of northern California. Elegantly integrated, the Cypress Club's lighting and design elements come together to create a soft, fluid, and lyrical space.

restaurants

project   **Cypress Club**
                San Francisco, CA

lighting   **Jordan Mozer**

architect   **Jordan Mozer**

interior   **Jordan Mozer**

photographer   **Dennis Anderson**

Pin spotlights provide accent lighting for tabletops, artwork, and displays.

r e s t a u r a n t s

project
**Beer Restaurant,
Aoyama City
Tokyo, Japan**
lighting
TL Yamagiwa Lab
interior
Masanori Umeda
photographer
Yoshio Shiratori

A shiny red counter slices the space like a Japanese sword. Whimsical "outer space" ceiling-mounted fixtures provide subtle downlighting.

project **Silks Restaurant,
Mandarin Oriental Hotel
San Francisco, CA**
lighting **Randall Whitehead and
Catherine Ng**
interior **James Marzo Design**
photographer **John Vaughan**

Recessed accent luminaires bring out the colors of the painting. The custom fixtures become part of the atmosphere, instead of overpowering or simply fading into the background.

project **Zenith Restaurant
Denver, CO**
lighting **Clanton Engineering**
interior **Gensler and Associates**
photographer **Marco Lorenzetti**

The main dining areas feature a gray carpet, white table linens, and black chairs. The walls are white polymix. Cove lighting in the ceiling shines down into the dining space through perforated metal panels. A cylinder penetrating a black disk forms a table that holds a dramatic display of flowers and desserts. Additional lighting in the dining area is from low-voltage lights on a cable system. The walls are a white polymix.

project	**Regina Chi Chi Beignet**
	San Francisco, CA
lighting	**Randall Whitehead,**
	Catherine Ng
architect	**Huntsman Associates**
interior	**Jessica Hall**
photographer	**Dennis Anderson**

Playful "cuckoo's nest" pendant fixtures by Christina Spann invite diners into the party-like atmosphere of this space. A framing projector creates a star pattern at the far end of the restaurant, the visual reward for making the long trip from the front door.

project **Longshoreman's Daughter Seattle, WA**
lighting **Brendt Markee**
architect **Rik Adams**
interior **Adams / Mohler Architects**
photographer **Robert Pisano**

In this overall view of the restaurant, Calder-like pendants soar above the tables. Light-colored disks act as reflectors to produce good ambient light.

project **Spot Bagel Bakery Wallingford Seattle, WA**
lighting **Adams / Mohler Architects**
architect **Rik Adams and Rick Mohler**
interior **Adams / Mohler Architects**
photographer **Steve Keating**

In the condiment area, pendants float above the tables and giant lava-lamp-topped sconces punctuate the bench.

project	**Spot Bagel Bakery**	This view of the seating area and spiral, sheet-metal column demonstrates how circline fluorescents help this "spaceship" lift off. Custom pendants of perforated metal and glowing rings are suspended over the bar, while huge, lava-lamp-topped luminaires hover over the tables.
	Newmark	
	Seattle, WA	
lighting	**Adams / Mohler Architects**	
architect	**Rik Adams and Rick Mohler**	
interior	**Adams / Mohler Architects**	
photographer	**Robert Pisano**	

Located near a busy pedestrian thoroughfare, a twelve-foot long, neon-lit fish sign attracts passersby. Bronze-colored mirrors and focused, high-key, low-voltage, cable-mounted lighting enhance the surroundings without distracting diners. The use of white plastic laminate and maple cabinets creates a sense of cleanliness, order, and simplicity.

A seismic frame at the back of this narrow space posed an aesthetic hurdle. A hole that echoes the shape of the frame was made in the back wall, and covered with metal mesh. Fixtures mounted to the sides illuminate the screen as a translucent element. A cable system does the accent lighting while pendants designed by Pam Morris add the glowing fill lights.

restaurants

project	**Azur Restaurant and Ballroom**
	Minneapolis, MN
lighting	**Michael DiBlasi**
architect	**Gregory Rothweiler**
interior	**Richard D'Amico, D'Amico and Partners, Inc.,**
	Gregory Rothweister, Shea Architects
photographer	**Christian Korab**

Theatrical pattern projectors and theatrical fixtures with colored gels light the fabric-draped
ceiling. Custom, double, glue-chipped and back-painted pendants are suspended between
sections of fabric. Paintings are accented with wall-mount picture lights.

project **Aqua Restaurant**
San Francisco, CA
lighting **Larry French**
architect **Frost and Tsuchi**
interior **Frost and Tsuchi**
photographer **Douglas A. Salin**

Architectural details flanking the huge mirrors throughout the space are subtly fore- and back-lighted to show off the textural quality of the wall surfaces. Individual votive candles produce pleasing islands of illumination at each table. The entry makes a subtle statement. The feeling is calming to the eye and sets up the anticipation of a sumptuous meal.

project	**The Backstage Restaurant**
	San Francisco, CA
lighting	**Terry Ohm**
photographer	**Charles Cormany**

Small Lightolier monopoints are used to highlight the ivory-colored columns surrounding the room. The steel sconces, formed in the shapes of ivy branches, emit a soft indirect light from behind each leaf. The balance of the lighting is achieved with custom-designed floor lamps and wall sconces to create the intimate atmosphere of a living room.

project	**P.F. Changs**
	China Bistro
	Scottsdale, AZ
lighting	**Pam Ackerman**
architect	**Rick Schreiber**
interior	**Ann McKenzie**
photographer	**Mark Boisclair**
	Photography, Inc.

Custom designed, floating, circular metal and canvas discs are suspended mysteriously over the dining floor. Low-voltage cable lights dash across space from statues to walls. Track lights float overhead like stars in the dark sky.

project   **Restaurant Lulu**
              San Francisco, CA
lighting   **David Malman,**
              Architectural Lighting Design
architect   **Cass Calder Smith Architecture**
interior   **Cass Calder Smith Architecture**
photographer   **Michael Bruk**

The side seating area is lit by a combination of reflected uplights on the back of each column. Paintings are illuminated with custom wall-mounted accent lights.

project   **Restaurant Lulu**
              San Francisco, CA
lighting   **Drawing: Elizabeth Nurre**
architect   **Cass Calder Smith Architecture**
interior   **Cass Calder Smith Architecture**
photographer   **Micheal Bruk**

Floor plan.

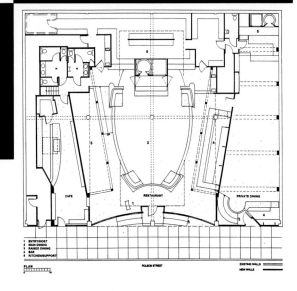

DAY FEBRUARY SIXTH
YOTE POINT BENEFIT

SEE DIANE OR NANCY
FOR TICKET INFORMATION

project	**JoAnn's B Street Cafe**
	San Mateo, CA
lighting	**Lloyd Fogelhut**
architect	**Lloyd Fogelhut**
interior	**Sady S. Hayashida**
photographer	**Dennis Anderson**

Peering through the front window, a full-size theater marquee fills the view. Customers are drawn in by the warm, fun feel of the diner, created by the bright lighting and the neon colors cast by the marquee.

project
Splendidos
San Francisco, CA
lighting sculpture designer
Pam Morris
architect
Pat Kuleto
interior
Pat Kuleto
photographer
Dennis Anderson

[right]   The color of the glass and incandescent light alludes to embers and coals, hearth and heart. The warm colors bring to mind torches, embers, or fires, and successfully convey the designer's concept of being in an ancient place lit by a flickering flame.

[bottom left]
The fixtures echo the restaurant's rustic hearty food.

[bottom right]   This exciting restaurant, located in a concrete structure filled with upscale stores and eateries, transports diners to an earlier place and time. The custom made light sculptures hint at lost civilizations, and the glowing embers left by a fire.

project   **Jimmy's American Place**
                Carmel, CA
lighting   **Donald Maxcy**
architect   **Donald Maxcy**
interior   **Kenny Fukumoto**
photographer   **Russell Abraham**

The dining area is highlighted by overhead lighting and subtle, colored glass gels slashing light through the glass blocks.

project   **BuckEye Roadhouse**
                Mill Valley, CA
lighting   **Lewis Rosenberg and**
                Alicia Jackson
architect   **Real Restaurants, Inc.**
interior   **Real Restaurants, Inc.**
photographer   **Doug Salin**

Custom faux-finished Italian pendant and sconce fixtures provide ambient light to the space. Recessed low-voltage fixtures highlight tables, mantles, booths, artwork, and a fieldstone fireplace.

41

restaurants

project	**Wizardz**
	Universal City, CA
lighting	**Communication Arts /**
	Gallegos Design
architect	**Ray Hirata**
interior	**Richard Foy,**
	Mike Doyle,
	Lydia Young
photographer	**Grey Crawford**

[right] Blacklighting, special effects lighting, and exotic fabrics create the right ambiance for clairvoyance at Wizardz restaurant.

[following page] This restaurant's main entry is pure theater, with signage that is illuminated moments before the doors open. Lights and words extinguish as the elevator goes up. A fiber-optic lightning bolt dramatizes the floor and creates a path to the elevator door.

project	**The Silver Diner**
	Towson, MD
lighting	**Charles Morris Mount**
architect	**Charles Morris Mount**
interior	**Charles Morris Mount**
photographer	**Doug Brown**

Cove ceilings, clad with pink boomerang laminate, reflect concealed neon, which enhances the color. This neon makes the polished stainless steel, used throughout the diner, feel warm and friendly. Downlights are a combination of MR16 and PAR 36 flood lamps. Three colors of neon (pink, red and white) run in metal coves fitted with moldings on the ceiling soffits. Incandescent pendant lamps over the counter further enhance a warm tone with their reflected uplighting on the ceiling.

ELEVATE
ARISE
UPLIFT
ASCEND
LEVITATE

WONDER

project
**McDonald's: A&S Center
New York, NY**
lighting
Charles Morris Mount
architect
Charles Morris Mount
interior
Charles Morris Mount
photographer
Norman McGrath

[left] The lighting in the space plays on variations of a jewel-tone palette; ruby, sapphire, and diamond, adding sparkle to the reflective interior finishes. Neon is used in a very architectural and graphic manner; bars, lines, squiggles, circles, and zigzags.

[below] The walls of the dining room are composed of colorful neon patterns placed behind panels of hand-cast ridged glass tiles, creating a kinetic wall sculpture. These panels illuminate the room and add fun to this fast-food restaurant. Colorful bands of neon on the ceiling add light and give subliminal guidelines to patrons. The illuminated walls are reflected in the polished aluminum accoustical ceiling panels, giving the illusion of height.

project
**Stardust Sangu
Restaurant
Osaka, Japan**
lighting
Stom Ushidate
architect
Robert R. Lowe
interior
Stom Ushidate
photographer
**Nacasa and
Partners Inc.**

The banquet seating has cove lights and downlights, to create a twinkling star effect. On each table, a polished chrome penlight candelabra helps further the illusion of sitting surrounded by stars.

project
**California Cafe
Bar & Grill
Fort Lauderdale, FL**
lighting
**Lewis Rosenberg,
Alicia Jackson**
architect
Jennifer Johanson
interior
**Eric Engstrom,
Barbara Wofling**
photographer
Dennis Anderson

The main level dining area offers views of the intracoastal waterway and marina. Special low-voltage cable lighting is interwoven with sculpture.

restaurants

project   **Postrio**
          San Francisco, CA
lighting   *lighting sculpture designer*
          Pam Morris;
          cable light with
          Frank Neidhardt
architect   **Pat Kuleto**
interior   **Pat Kuleto**
photographer   **Dennis Anderson**

Hovering glass orbs of shadow, light, and color
greet diners as they wait for their tables. This
restaurant's layout presented difficult challenges:
To reach the main dining room, patrons needed
to be drawn through a narrow bar area and
down a staircase. The neon fixture, whose exotic
hue is produced by blending three different colors
of light behind a face plate, draws patrons to the
entrance of the dining room.

project
Enoteca Del Fornaio
San Diego, CA
lighting
Backen Arrigoni
and Ross Architects
architect
Backen Arrigoni
and Ross Architects
interior
Backen Arrigoni
and Ross Architects
photographer
Douglas A. Salin

The design concept was to create an outside room that was comfortable for dining, and, at the same time, attention-getting to passers by. The signage was uplighted with neon. By hiding the light source behind a facia, the lettering predominates instead of the neon itself. A white neon underlights the bar and serving area, against a clean backdrop of white tile. A band of yellow neon underlines the name and plays off the mustard-colored wall finish.

restaurants

project
Chops
Atlanta, GA
lighting sculpture designer
Pam Morris
architect
Pat Kuleto
interior
Pat Kuleto
photographer
Alan McGee

Custom-designed sconces and pendants glisten against the rich wood interiors.

project   **Granita**
              Malibu, CA
lighting   *lighting sculpture designer*
              Pam Morris
architect   **Ben Burkhalter and**
              Barbara Lazaroff
interior   **Barbara Lazaroff**
photographer   **Martin Fine**

Color and light are interrelated and, when blended
properly, make both people and food look their
best. Recessed accent light brings out the colors in
the floor, columns, and paintings; soft, diffuse
lighting warms the restaurant's undulating curves.

project   **Granita**
              Malibu, CA
lighting   *lighting sculpture designer*
              Pam Morris
architect   **Ben Burkhalter and**
              Barbara Lazaroff
interior   **Barbara Lazaroff**
photographer   **Martin Fine**

Granita uses both ambient and decorative,
hand-blown light sculptures to create a
sophisticated atmosphere.

project   **Sapphire Mynx Bistro**
              Sebastopol, CA
lighting   *lighting fixture designer*
              Christina Spann / Lightspann
architect   **Dave Leff Construction**
              and Paul Carara
interior   **Paul Carara**
photographer   **Terrance Mc Carthy**

Inspired by the bistro's name, Sapphire Mynx, Lightspann
designed a series of deep-blue blown glass orbs to illuminate
and define the area around the bar.

project **Granita**
Malibu, CA

lighting *lighting sculpture designer*
Pam Morris

architect **Ben Barkhalter and**
Barbara Lazaroff

interior **Barbara Lazaroff**

photographer **Martin Fine**

Barbara Lazaroff has designed an incredibly beautiful restaurant that combines soft, diffused lighting, undulating curves, and hand-blown glass light sculptures by Pam Morris of Exciting Lighting.

HOTELS

sumptuous satisfaction for guests

Hotels can represent the ultimate lighting challenge. The objective is two-fold: first, to make guests feel at home, so they can relax and be comfortable, second, to create areas of dramatic visual interest—so that people will be attracted to and impressed with the surroundings. Lighting sets the tone for the whole environment: from the building entryway to the guest suites and bathrooms, it is the critical element in creating a first-class hotel atmosphere.

Lighting of outside areas, building facades, and signage must be carefully designed to help lead patrons into the building. Too often, one drives into a large hotel complex, or walks down a street toward one, and it is not readily apparent where to enter the building or how to get to the registration desk. This design flaw is easily corrected through proper lighting. A subtle splash of light around the entrance will naturally draw people's attention. Highlighting the reception area will attract traffic in that direction.

These techniques don't have to be flashy, they can remain unobtrusive and well-integrated into the overall design.

Hotel suites themselves should have lighting that is similar to residential lighting, with comfort and convenience the key factors in the design. Ambient light, reflected from walls and ceilings, should be the main light source in the room. Wall sconces and torchieres are a good way to achieve this effect. Table lamps can be used, but

should have opaque shades to eliminate glare. Indirect lighting will give rooms soft, comfortable, but adequate illumination, which will allow people to work or relax without distraction.

Bath lighting is also very important. The way a guest feels is strongly affected by how they see themselves in the mirror. For task light at the vanity, use fixtures flanking the mirror, to evenly illuminate the entire face. Fixtures mounted above the

mirror cast unflattering shadows, making people look tired and older than they really are. The rule of thumb, especially for hotels, is to always put people in their best light.

Because hotel projects require a tiered lighting approach, successful hotel lighting is really at the cutting edge; demonstrating how remarkably far the hospitality industry and its designers will go to create the perfect retreat.

project **St. Regis Hotel, New York, NY**

lighting **Gustin Tan, Brennan Beer Gorman Monk / Interiors**
Theo Kondos, T. Kondos Associates

architect **Julia F. Monk, Brennan Beer Gorman Monk / Interiors**

interior **David W. Beer, Brennan Beer Gorman Monk / Interiors**

photographer **Anthony P. Albarello**

In lighting the exterior of the original building, the design team sought to highlight the windows and carved Indiana limestone. On the small balconies flanking the sides of the old building, 35-watt high-pressure sodium lamps provide uplighting. At the third level, 400-watt lamps highlight the three-level architectural element where the next molding occurs. Two hundred and fifty-watt lamps light the roof from the 15th and 16th floors.

project
The Governor Hotel
Portland, OR

lighting
Candra Scott

architect
Candra Scott

interior architect
Candra Scott and
The Malder Company

interior
Candra Scott

photographer
Langdon Clay

[previous page]
The lobby area features a larger-than-life size mural of Lewis and Clark's journey from Celilo Falls down the Columbia to Fort Clatsop, and Sacajawea overlooking the ocean as she saw it for the first time. Custom designed furniture with hand-painted feather and diamond motifs, taken from the original architectural details, continues this theme in the 100 guest rooms. Leaf patterns decorate both the column-based standing lamps and massive, hanging fixtures.

The Manhattan Tokyo Japan

The design inspiration for this 130-room luxury hotel evolved both from the hotel's name, The Manhattan, and from its architectural design, which recalls the silhouette of the Chrysler Building in New York City.

The design team, headed by Candra Scott, decided to recreate the glamour of New York City from the mid-1920s until 1940. Many months of research on the Art Deco period were necessary to produce authentically-designed interiors, as well as to locate original Art Deco furniture and lighting fixtures for the project.

The lobby combines period lighting and furniture with luxurious, custom-designed pieces from the 1925 Paris Exhibition. Light falling on the rich palette of soft greens, golds, and reds creates a feeling of warmth and comfort.

The hotel's restaurant was inspired by the famous Parisian brasserie La Coupole. The room's many columns are illuminated with a soft wash of light from lamps hidden in the molding below. Recessed can lights in the ceiling wash three large murals depicting *The Grand Voyage*. The original chandeliers are vintage from the Ziegfeld. Designed to mimic the style of an elegant New York mansion, the room's rich wood tones and luxuriously upholstered golden walls reflect light warmly and create a beautiful setting for any occasion.

Accurate period style follows through into every space of the hotel. The Parlor is influenced by small smoking rooms found in hotels and theaters of the period. Ceiling lights are recessed in a soffit to accent the copper leaf ceiling. Can lights wash light over murals and the Parlor's cork-banded walls. Thirties-vintage floor lamps of chrome and green glass offer task lighting, without marring the carefully created fantasy.

The interior decoration of the hospitality suites, like the rest of the hotel, hides functionality behind luxury. The Humphrey Bogart suite has a tailored, 1940s style, with recessed can lights in a coffered ceiling, and paneling in deep, rich tones of mahogany. The Greta Garbo quarters contains floor lamps with black and gold painted bases and alabaster bowl tops. Stunning jewel tones throughout the room portray the opulence of Paris in the 1930s. The Bette Davis suite honors the ultimate grande dame with the richness and warmth of a traditional mansion, including matching chandeliers and sconces, and floor lamps with carved, gold leaf bases.

Since the rooms on this floor are very popular for small receptions and business meetings, it was especially important that they have an intimate, residential atmosphere. The lighting is designed to create an overall, ambient glow, while providing task light above the conference and dining tables.

hotels

project	**The Manhattan Chiba, Japan**
lighting	**Paul Marantz, Kaoru Mende**
interior architect	**Candra Scott**
interior	**Candra Scott**
photographer	**Yoshiteru Baba**

The lobby combines original Art Deco lighting and furniture, as well as luxurious custom designed pieces from the 1925 Paris exhibition. The rich palette of soft greens, golds, and reds creates a feeling of warmth and comfort. Recessed spot lighting strengthens the illusion that light is streaming from the painting on the wall. Dramatic uplighting enhances architectural features.

project	**The Governor Hotel Portland, OR**
lighting	**Candra Scott**
architect	**Candra Scott**
interior	**Candra Scott and The Malder Company**
interior	**Candra Scott**
photographer	**Langdon Clay**

The artwork for the guestrooms was inspired by Lewis and Clark's journal illustrating nature, flora, and fauna. Each guest room door is appointed with an Indian wall sconce, which throws a romantic "torch" light. Painted feather and diamond motifs, taken from the original architectural details, continues this theme in the 100 guest rooms. leaf patterns decorate both the column-based standing lamps and massive, hanging fixtures.

project	**Palace of the Lost City Sun City, South Africa**
lighting	**Ross De Alessi**
architect	**Wimberly Allison Tong & Goo**
interior	**Wilson & Associates**
photographer	**Courtesy of Sun International**

In the porte-cochère entry to The Palace of the Lost City sculpture and architectural features are lit from beneath to create a fantastic, theatrical effect.

project	**Palace of the Lost City Sun City, South Africa**
lighting	**Ross De Alessi**
architect	**Wimberly Allison Tong & Goo**
interior	**Wilson & Associates**
photographer	**Courtesy of Sun International**

In the "Elephant Court" doorway and balcony lighting evokes a torch lit Eastern Palace.

project
**Plaza Las Fuentes
Hotel
Pasadena, CA**
architect
Moore Rubell Yudell
interior
Babey-Moulton, Inc.
photographer
Jaime Ardiles Arce

Massive hanging chandeliers dominate the aesthetics of this passage, providing the general illumination and an intriguing design element. Seating groups are each in the warm light of a large table lamp. Lit upper balconies create definition and add perspective to the space.

project **Hyatt Regency San Francisco, CA**

lighting *principal designers* **Patricia Glasow and Len Auerbach** *lighting designer* **Virva Kokkonen**

architect **ELS / Elbasoni & Logan Architects**

interior **Hirsch / Bedner Associates**

photographer **John Sutton Photography**

[above]   The Cate uses a low-voltage open conductor wire system spanning up to 60 feet. Twenty-watt narrow spot MR16 lamps illuminate tables, plants, and artwork, as well as the stepped ceiling above the atrium floor.

[right]   Grazing light accents walls, foliage, and elevator shafts in the atrium. PAR64 spotlights define pedestrian paths and sculpture.

project   **The Triton Hotel**
              San Francisco, CA
lighting   **Terry Ohm**
architect   **Wil Wong**
interior   **Michael Moore**
photographer **John Vaughan**

The torchiere, fabricated from brushed steel, offers a contrast of whimsical lines with an industrial edge, creating an environment that offers both comfort and visual stimulation to the Triton's visitors.

project **Holiday Inn Express Osaka Utsubo Park Osaka, Japan**
lighting **Yukio Oka**
architect **Kazuhiro Motomochi**
interior **Kazuhiro Motomochi**
photographer **Atelier Fukumoto**

[left] Pass-through lighting is provided by the incandescent downlights. The designer created these unique sandblasted torchieres, which illuminate the fresco painting on the ceiling and also help create diffuse, inviting light for the space.

[below] Punch lighting is provided through a series of incandescent downlights. Attractive indirect lighting comes from the cove and the soffit. The designer created the unusual olive leaf-shaped fixtures for the walls and ceiling. The fixtures help to convey the hotel's theme, which is based on ancient Greek myths.

project **Dai Ichi Hotel Tokyo, Tokyo, Japan**
lighting **Naomi Miller, Bradley A. Bouch, Takae Oyake, Luminae Souter Lighting Design**
architect **Mitsubishi Estate Co., Ltd.**
interior **Media Five Limited**
photograher **Courtesy of Lutron**

Neon and fiber-optic lighting allow for special effects ranging from a simulated star field to a midnight-blue sky effect. Fluorescent wall-slot fixtures highlight the simulated outdoor trompe l'oeil wall. Recessed incandescent fixtures provide the ambient light, and decorative pendants, wall sconces and table lamps provide ambient light, style, and elegance to the interiors.

project	**Palace Ai Yahata**
	Fukuoka, Japan
lighting	**Kenji Kitani, Kousaku Matsumoto**
architect	**Seiji Tanaka, Ikuei Ikeda**
interior	**Seiji Tanaka, Hiroshi Kawaguchi**
photographer	**Masaaki Fukumoto**

The entrance is designed to create a South Seas island feeling. During the day it is bright, with natural light and glass that evokes the blue colors of the sea. At night, it has a very different look, as a "starry sky" emerges.

59

project
Grand Hyatt Bali
Bali, Indonesia
lighting
Jeff Miller
architect
Sydney C.L. Char,
Wimberly Allison Tong & Goo;
Naokazu Hanadoh
and Kazubiko Kuroka,
Shimizu Corp.
interior
Hirsh Bedner & Associates
photographer
Donna Day

The architects wanted a design that fit
unobtrusively into the fragile environment of
the island of Bali, and were inspired by the
Balinese village. Buildings with courtyards were
decentralized for an intimate setting. In this
dawn view through the entry colonades,
luminaires atop the columns provide a soft fill
light, in keeping with the intimate atmosphere.
The reception building is designed to resemble
a Balinese water palace.

project   **Granlibakken Resort**
            Tahoe City, CA
lighting   **Randall Whitehead**
architect   **Jeffrey A. Lundahl**
            Todd B. Lankenau
interior   **Sylvia Stevens**
photographer **Donna Kempner**

A plain T-bar grid ceiling with two- by four-foot
fluorescent lights was proposed for this conference
center. An imaginative redesign by the project
architect produced this stepped coffer detail using
dimmable color-corrected fluorescent lamps.
The three dimensional theme is picked up by semi-
circular sconces "floating" on mirrors, creating an
illusion of depth and space.

project   **Resort at Squaw Creek**
            Squaw Creek, CA
lighting   **Bradley A. Bouch,**
            Jim Benya,
            Luminae Souter
            Lighting Design
architect   **Ward Young Architects**
interior   **Simon Martin – Vegue**
            Winkelstein Moris
photographer **Chas McGrath**

Entering the lobby, the indoor space echoes nature's
colors on a warmer, more human scale. The designers
underscored the inherent opulence of the natural
materials, which include flame granite in the floors,
granite boulders taken from the site, and rough-hewn
Douglas fir framed chairs. Recessed spotlights create
sculptural shadows on the massive stone columns,
while hanging fixtures create pools of light to lead
patrons toward the information desk.

project
**Hyatt Regency
San Francisco
International Airport
Burlingame, CA**
lighting
**Mark Hornberger,
Hornberger & Worstell and
Vladimir Bazjanac, Ph.D.**
architect
Jack J. Worstell
interior
Architectural Interiors
photographer
Sally Painter

[left] A translucent, teflon-coated fiberglass fabric roof stretches across the 39,000 square foot atrium space. Natural light filters through the translucent fabric, providing ideal daylighting conditions for tree growth, and diffuse, ambient lighting for hotel functions.

[below] Subtly lit columns make this an intimate setting within the atrium. Accent lights mounted on the overlapping grid highlight the tables and plants.

project
**Bally's Hotel and Casino
Atlantic City, NJ**
lighting
**Naomi Miller,
Bradley A. Bouch,
Luminae Souter Lighting Design**
architect
William Tabler and Associates
interior
Joszi Meskan Associates
photographer
Peter Vitale

The use of color and the play of light from the reflective surfaces sets a "fantasy" mood. As guests proceed towards the registration desk, playful lighted columns, simulated sky lighting, and an oversized chandelier continue the experience.

project   **Post Ranch Inn
              Big Sur, CA**
lighting   **Linda Ferry**
architect   **G.K. Muennig**
interior   **Janet Gay Freed**
photographer **Douglas Salin**

The design team's challenge for the Post Ranch Inn was to make each room a private, intimate retreat. The light sources had to blend with the highly unique architecture, but not detract from the spectacular Pacific Ocean views. The majority of the room's light is ambient, created by several custom designed incandescent uplights. The uplights reflect light off a sculptural, curved wood ceiling, drawing out the natural tones of the wood. Low-voltage cable lights provide accent light. Three swing-arm lamps serve as reading lights for the bed and seating.

project   **Izumigo Plaza Hotel**
lighting   **Kaoru Mende, Hideto Mori**
architect   **Shimizu Corporation**
photographer **Lighting Planners Associates Inc.**

This wedding-oriented hotel and leisure facility, including tennis courts, features a church at the core of an elegant resort. Lighting inside the church is constantly coordinated with the outside. A spotlight lights up the church steeple from a distance. Pole lights, designed after a windmill, surround the church. Depending on the season, seven different kinds of illumination are operated inside the church. In the winter, the inside of the church glows with a blue light.

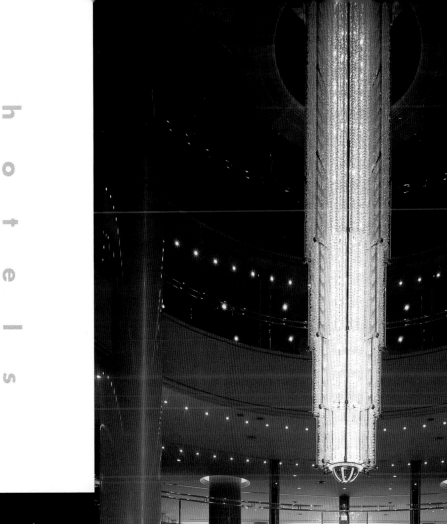

project
Nankai South Tower Hotel
Osaka, Japan
lighting
Kenji Kitani, Kousaku Matsumoto
architect
Ryuichi Yokogawa
interior
Yoshio Shibata, Saburo Morishima
photographer
Matsushita Electric Works, Ltd.

This breathtaking six-floor atrium has a luxurious
atmosphere. The eight-meter, two-ton chandelier is
designed with the motif of a South Seas island.
Incandescent light sources are located inside the
chandelier.

project
Hotel New Otani Makuhari
Chiba, Japan
lighting
Kenji Kitani,
Kousaku Matsumoto
architect
Ryuichi Yokogawa
interior
Yoshio Shibata,
Saburo Morishima,
Mikio Furusawa
photographer
Maasaki Fukumoto

The Japanese concept throughout the hotel
includes large pendant fixtures that evoke
Shojii screens, to create a comfortable,
warm, welcome feeling in the lobby.

63

project   **Hotel New Otani
Garden Court
Tokyo, Japan**
lighting   **Motoko Ishii**
architect   **Taisei Corporation**
photographer   **Akihisa Masuda**

The Garden Court has a new entrance with a
32-meter-tall atrium, topped with a light sculpture
designed in the image of a gemstone of light.
The light source consists of 17 50-watt, high-color
performance sodium lamps, with ten 20-watt red,
blue, and green colored fluorescent lamps, which
change color according to the clock, illuminating
the intervals.

hotels

project   **Dai Ichi Hotel
Tokyo Seafort
Tokyo, Japan**
lighting   **Shunji Tamai**
architect   **RIA Company, Ltd.**
interior   **MHS Planners
Architects & Engineers**
photographer   **Masami Sato**

Japanese-style wedding space in the hotel. Lighting
highlights the altar, and bride and groom stand;
the rest of the area is dimmed down.

project
**Disney's Wilderness Lodge
Lake Buena Vista, FL**
lighting
**Chip Israel,
Lighting Design Alliance**
architect
**Peter Dominick,
Urban Design Group**
photographer
Dan Forer, Forer, Inc.

This awe inspiring lobby includes 15-foot, decorative teepee lanterns with an internal glow and MR16 downlights to softly illuminate the floor. Quartz uplights mounted above the chandeliers create the perception of uplight from the chandeliers and throw a wash of light across the log ceiling. Typical corridors use compact fluorescent lamps in themed fixtures. Arts-and-Crafts-styled floor and table lamps provide pedestrian lighting at the floor level.

65

HOUSES OF WORSHIP

It is distressing to walk into a beautiful church, temple, or cathedral and find an inspiring interior that no one can appreciate because the lighting is so poorly done! Spiritual sanctuaries seem to suffer the most from incorrect illumination, because their sensitive designs can easily be lost amid glaring lights, or dark corners and ceilings. Stained-glass windows are almost always neglected, which is especially unfortunate since the possibilities are endless for increasing their visual presence through the use of lighting.

A soft glow of ambient illumination is particularly important in a spiritual gathering place, where the atmosphere can easily be shattered by invasive down-lights or spotlights. Gentle fill light can, at the same time, serve to illuminate ceilings and walls, and to bring out delicate detailing and woodwork carvings. It also can be bright enough to provide illumination for parishioners to read songs, prayers, or scripture. Too often, harsh downlights are used for this purpose; a poor choice, since down-lights tend to glare and can actually make reading more difficult. Downlights also cast unflattering shadows on people's faces.

As lighting designers we lament, *why go to the trouble of creating sublimely beautiful atmospheric effects if they are lit too poorly for people to see?* Even the most humble church setting benefits from artful lighting, to enhance the visitor's experience of worship.

Theatrical lighting tech-niques are useful for lighting a house of worship, where lighting serves many of the same functions as in a theater: there must be adequate ambient light for the audience, the key players must be high-lighted, and the set must be carefully illuminated, so that it is apparent without over-shadowing the people.

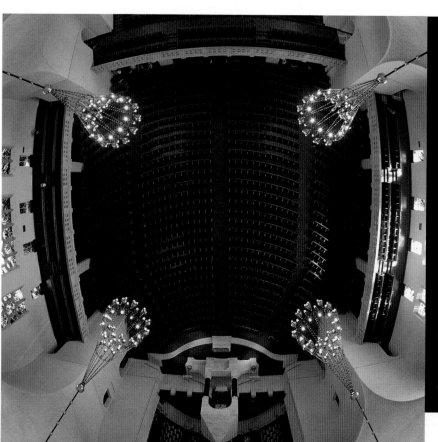

project
**Temple Emanu El Sanctuary
San Francisco, CA**
lighting
**Len Auerbach
Larry French**
architect
David Robinson
photographer
Bob Swanson

[left] Although the chandeliers deliver a considerable amount of general light into the room, the quality is so even that the surfaces tended to flatten. In particular, the dome interior was so generally lit that the sense of a curved surface receding from the viewer was lost. Along with complete cleaning, rewiring, and relamping, custom uplight fixtures were added around the interior perimeter of the lower band of each chandelier.

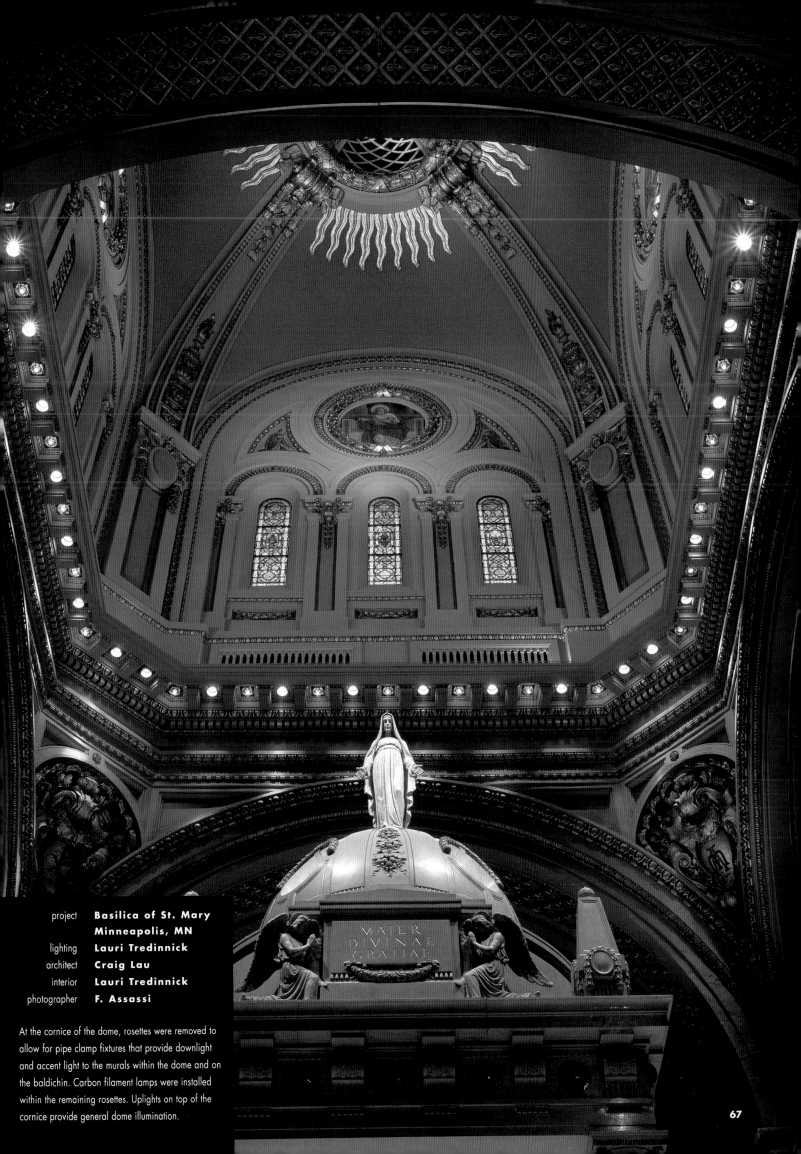

project **Basilica of St. Mary**
Minneapolis, MN
lighting **Lauri Tredinnick**
architect **Craig Lau**
interior **Lauri Tredinnick**
photographer **F. Assassi**

At the cornice of the dome, rosettes were removed to allow for pipe clamp fixtures that provide downlight and accent light to the murals within the dome and on the baldichin. Carbon filament lamps were installed within the remaining rosettes. Uplights on top of the cornice provide general dome illumination.

St. Stephen's Church Belvedere California

St. Stephen's Church has a ceiling with a 40-foot peak. When its parishioners painted the aging concrete vault an azure blue that no one could see from the ground, they realized it would take more than paint to lighten up the atmosphere.

The cast concrete church structure was built in 1953. Its original wiring ran through the walls in conduits that accommodated a maximum of five circuits for the lighting of the 80-foot by 30-foot ceiling space. The original lighting—rows of 300-watt PAR 38 lamps in porcelain sockets running in a wooden trough between the columns—pointed down from 20 feet, leaving the ceiling in darkness.

When the congregation decided to bring light to the newly painted ceiling, they called in lighting designer Randall Whitehead. His challenge was to solve the lighting problem within the power limitations imposed by the structure, and to find a

way to hide any new wiring in a poured concrete building. The designer created a system that allows members to light the church in a variety of ways for different times and purposes.

The existing trough is fitted with a new bottom and recessed adjustable fixtures, using 90-watt PAR quartz lamps directed toward the walls. The design extends wiring from the troughs down the columns, hiding it in the routed back of a trim board stained gray to match the concrete. Halfway down each column, about ten feet from the floor, the designer installed custom luminaires that provide uplighting and downlighting at the same time. Uplighting comes from 250-watt, 4100 Kelvin metal halide sources, and downlighting from 150-watt R40 blue filtered incandescent "jeweler's lamps" with a color temperature close to that of the metal halide.

The three adjustable, 45-watt quartz PAR 38 lamps are mounted on the wall near the floor to accent the Christ figure. The incandescents,

whether dimmed to a reddish hue, or turned up to a more golden glow, offer a pointed contrast to the rest of the lighting. Trough fixtures, accent lights, and downlights can be dimmed manually, and there is a separate switching for the uplights. This flexible system can create variations of intimacy and loftiness, with illumination from selective to full.

The previous system consumed 9,000 watts; it provided eight to ten foot-candles to the pews, and no light at all to the ceiling. The new system uses 6,000 watts and, when all the lights are operating at maximum intensity, provides about 32 foot-candles at the pews. The dimming feature makes for long lamp life, as well as variable kinds of ambiance.

The total project came in under budget which naturally pleased the parishioners. Their greatest pleasure, however, is the effect on their windows. For the first time in the 42-year history of the church, the stained-glass windows can be seen from the outside at night.

project **St. Stephen's Church Belvedere, CA**
lighting **Randall Whitehead**
architect **Harold Hansen**
photographer **Ben Janken**

[above] Thanks to a new lighting design plan, the stained glass windows of the church can be seen at night.

[below] This schematic drawing, shown to the parishioners, depicts how the new wall sconces would be mounted to the columns. The top view shows the compact metal halide source, located in the upper half of the luminaire.

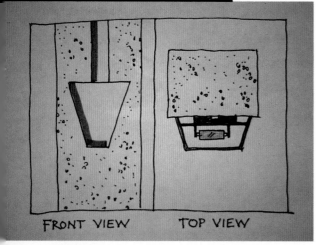

FRONT VIEW   TOP VIEW

project **St. Stephen's Church**
        Belvedere, CA

lighting **Randall Whitehead**

architect **Harold Hansen**

photographer **Ben Janken**

Custom wall sconces, lamped with compact metal halide sources pointed upward, and color-corrected incandescent R40 lamps pointed downward, create a dramatic, yet humanizing overall effect.

project **St. Stephen's Church
Belvedere, CA**
lighting **Randall Whitehead**
architect **Harold Hansen**
photographer **Ben Janken**

The metal halide lamps inside the sconces do an excellent job of showing off the ceiling details and providing a crisp overall illumination.

h o u s e s   o f

w o r s h i p

project **Durham Cathedral
England, UK**
lighting **Graham Phoenix**
architect **Ian Curry**
photographer **Chris Arthur**

Lighting of the choir showing the highlighting of the Neville screen behind the high altar.

project **Durham Cathedral
England, UK**
lighting **Graham Phoenix**
architect **Ian Curry**
photographer **Chris Arthur**

The scheme comprises a large number of projectors mounted in the galleries, using mainly 300-watt tungsten halogen sources with a choice of five different lenses, varying from very narrow to very wide. Downlighting on the pews provides the practical illumination. This is balanced by the high-lighting of the architecture including the face of the triforium and the main piers of the arcade.

project **Durham Cathedral**
 England, UK
lighting **Graham Phoenix**
architect **Ian Curry**
photographer **Chris Arthur**

The creation of mutiple lighting elements enables the
cathedral to be presented and experienced under
many different lighting conditions. The lighting control
system employs techniques similar to those used in
stage lighting. Control is achieved through the use of
dimmers and a computer-based control with
pre-programmed scenes. The system allows the full
cathedral to be lit for grand services, or the choir
area alone may be lit for smaller, evening functions.

71

project	**Church of Our Lady of Loretto**
	Notre Dame, IN
lighting	**William C. Lam**
architect	**Woollen, Molzan and Partners, Inc.**
interior	**Woollen, Molzan and Partners, Inc.**
photographer	**Balthazar Korab**

A transparent acoustical reflector in the Church of Our Lady of Loretto at Notre Dame is used to integrate the lighting and sound systems. It allows lighting scenes to be created for different liturgical events.

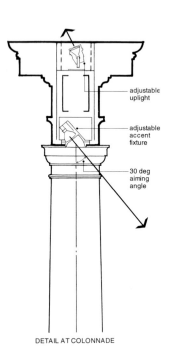

adjustable uplight

adjustable accent fixture

30 deg aiming angle

DETAIL AT COLONNADE

[left] In addition to lighting attached to the new acoustical reflector, a colonnade conceals uplighting for the murals, as well as task and accent lighting for the space.

[right] Use of fixtures on this 25-foot diameter ring allows "theater in the round" lighting for events.

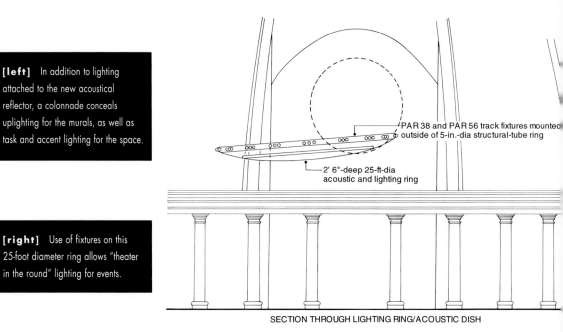

PAR 38 and PAR 56 track fixtures mounted outside of 5-in.-dia structural-tube ring

2' 6"-deep 25-ft-dia acoustic and lighting ring

SECTION THROUGH LIGHTING RING/ACOUSTIC DISH

project	**Duquette Pavillion**
	San Francisco, CA
lighting	**Tony Duquette**
architect	**Tony Duquette**
interior	**Tony Duquette**
photographer	**Douglas A. Salin**

[top] The Ducquette Pavillion is a place of magic and quiet wonder. The multi-layered lighting system adds a tremendous sense of depth to the altar area. The two green urns are illuminated from within so that the gossamer leaves glow. The metallic trees, too, have an interior illumination that energizes the senses. Theatrical fixtures hidden behind the arched proscenium do a spectacular job of bringing the sunburst to life, while hundreds of candles surround the figure of Saint John.

[bottom] Well-integrated lighting enhances the inspiring art and architectural detailing. Warm-colored lamps play up the sheen of the metal surfaces.

73

project
Temple Emanu El Sanctuary
San Francisco, CA
lighting
Len Auerbach, Larry French
architect
David Robinson
photographer
Bob Swanson

Surrounding the choir are large ornamental
that frame the tabernacle area. The individu
grille sections are defined by double column
support the arching top of each grille. Becau
the deep relief ornamentation and gold leaf
the grilles are illuminated with a grazing lig
emphasize the architectural shape.

project
**Temple Emanu El Sanctuary
San Francisco, CA**
lighting
Len Auerbach, Larry French
architect
David Robinson
photographer
Bob Swanson

[top left] The design of this decorative opening is based upon an early Maybeck composition and provides an excellent location for supplemental lighting. General downlighting of the congregation floor is installed in the oculus: 1000-watt PAR64 medium flood fixtures increase lighting levels for reading prayer books. A combination of very narrow, 6-volt PAR64 spotlights and theatrical ellipsoidal 1000-watt spots accent the side altar areas and focus dramatically on the central altar and the sanctuary.

[bottom left] Housed beneath the architectural canopy located behind the altar is the English-crafted Ark of the Covenant. The Ark is a central focus of worship because it contains the Torah, the holy scripture of the Jewish faith. Previously unlit, the cloisonne exterior of the Ark is now illuminated by very small MR16 fixtures located high within the canopy and out of sight of the congregation. These luminaires also add supplemental lighting at the bench where the scriptures are read.

[below] A detail shot of the retrofitted original fixtures in the hallways.

h o u s e s   o f
w o r s h i p

75

project	**Basilica Nuestra**	Dimmable halogen sources were
	Señora del Pilar	chosen for their color rendition,
	Argentina	which complements the other,
lighting	**Leonor Bedel and Associates**	more traditional, incandescent
architect	**Primoli y Blanqui**	sources in the church.
photographer	**Hector y Jorge Verdecchia**	

project	**Basilica Nuestra**	The Basilica Del Pilar is located
	Señora del Pilar	in the historic district of the city.
	Argentina	Great care was taken to install
lighting	**Leonor Bedel and Associates**	lighting that provides adequate
architect	**Primoli y Blanqui**	illumination without overpowering
photographer	**Hector y Jorge Verdecchia**	the existing decorative fixtures.

houses of
worship

project
Congregation Shalom
Fox Point, WI
lighting
Steven L. Klein, principal; Lana Nathe
architect
Torke Wirth & Pujara
interior
Studios of Potente
photographer
Mark F. Heffron

[top] Six pairs of torsioned conductor cables span the width of the lightwell. Miniature mirror reflector floods are carefully aimed to avoid lamp flash, as viewed from the congregation. Eighty lamps backlight the 45-foot wide by 35-foot high windows.

[bottom] The "Tree of Life" is a powerful symbol of faith and inspiration for worship at Congregation Shalom. The lighting design is a subtle catalyst enhancing the relationship between art, architecture, and the profound nature of spiritual congregation. The window, a 28-foot high by 45-foot wide custom glass sculpture, is the center from which the entire design radiates, and the focal point of the sanctuary. The highly textured masonry wall flanking the window is grazed by concealed downlights using 75PAR30 lamps to evoke memories of the Wailing Wall in Jerusalem.

project	**Western Presbyterian Church**	The softly lit plaza facade
	Washington, D.C.	shows off dramatic highlights,
lighting	**George Sexton Associates**	from in-ground quartz
architect	**KressCox Associates**	uplights, and sparkle from
interior	**KressCox Associates**	glowing stained glass
photographer	**Max McKenzie**	windows lit from within.

SHOWROOMS AND DISPLAY

drawing on dynamic impact

Showrooms depend on properly designed lighting, and on creating the right atmosphere to make the merchandise or product look enticing. In a showroom, more than any other place, the lighting effects must be spectacular—patrons expect to see products presented dramatically. Thus, accent lighting takes center stage, but this does not mean that ambient lighting can be ignored: these two aspects of lighting design must blend together to create a visual balance.

The ambient lighting should be sumptuous, filling large showroom spaces with soft illumination that lets the room seem lofty without being intimidating. Very often, much of the potential drama in a grand room is missed because the architecture is not given enough emphasis by the lighting design. Well-designed lighting brings out the best aspects of a space's architectural assets. Accent lighting can then enhance those wonderful touches by adding depth, dimension, and, above all, drama.

The lighting in a showroom can be more daring than lighting in a retail space, but the essentials still remain the same: people need to be illuminated as well as architecture, and the lighting should not overpower the room. In showrooms, light must still play the role of a servant to the customers, art, and architecture, rather than that of the master, commanding all the attention.

project	San Francisco Mart
	San Francisco, CA
lighting	Randall Whitehead
architect	Linda Hinrichs
interior	Linda Hinrichs
photographer	Donna Kempner

Black lights punch up neon-bright colors in this surrealistic display.

project	**Pool House, San Francisco, CA**
lighting	**Becca Foster**
architect	**Steve Geiszler and Ken Rupel**
interior	**Steve Geiszler and Ken Rupel**
photographer	**Sharon Risedorph**

These fixtures have deeply saturated color filters to wash brushed-aluminum panels in bright colors. Pool luminaires were re-lamped and colored gels were added to extend the colors below water, creating the illusion that the panels continue deeply below the surface.

project
Chrysler Technology Center, Styling Dome Auburn Hills, MI
lighting
Stefan Graf, Illuminart Mojtaba Navaab, University of Michigan
architect
CRSS Architects, Inc.
interior
CRSS Architects, Inc.
photographer
Balthazar Korab

Red and blue theatrical filters, along with dichroics and gobos, can turn the simulation dome into a whirring blur of colors and shapes. The gobos also have more practical uses. Engineers can use the leaf pattern to simulate how a car looks parked under a tree, and one of the patterns is the Chrysler logo.

Chrysler Technology Center Michigan

For Chrysler's three-million square-foot Technology Center in Michigan, lighting designer Stefan Graf was faced with enormous challenges. This one-billion-dollar center for car designers, engineers, and those in charge of marketing and purchase of materials was created as the place where 7,000 employees coordinate work on design and engineering. The styling dome is the highlight of the center. The dome is a fully enclosed part of the building that can serve as a facility for company officers, a press preview area for new models, and a meeting place for directors reviewing product design.

The dome has a programmable, direct and indirect lighting system. The designers can see the new models in controlled conditions that simulate the outdoors when outdoor viewing is inhibited by weather. The dome has three turntables for display models, and an 80-foot wide projection screen that can be lowered into the floor. The dome's up-to-date acoustic features include perforated metal panels that absorb excess sound.

Naturally, lighting was a prime concern because of the huge visual impact it can have on product evaluation. This design allows for computer-controlled changes in light quality, quantity, pattern, and color.

Luminaries are installed behind 14-inch wide retractable perforated aluminum disks, placed to highlight the contours and features of cars on the floor; 85 lamps can illuminate up to 21 cars with 5600 degrees Kelvin metal halide light. The color rendering index (CRI) of this light closely approaches that of the sun.

The luminaires have motorized mirrors that allow a 360 degree rotation of the beam. Adjustments can be made in beam size, beam edge (hard or soft) and templates to create special effects patterns that simulate various shadows in outdoor lighting conditions.

Mojtaba Navvab of University of Michigan's architecture, planning, and research laboratory provided the light angles necessary for even illumination of the surface of the dome. Dome and cove walls are illuminated using a combination of compact fluorescents, metal halide, and filtered quartz lamps, located both on the floor and the top of the cove walls.

Compact fluorescent lamps illuminate the lower areas of the dome, while metal halide and quartz lamps provide light for the center and upper areas. The quartz and compact fluorescents help compensate for the metal halides' four-minute warm up time. The other lamps actually dim at the same rate that the metal halides come up, so the illumination is consistent.

project	**Chrysler Technology Center, Styling Dome**
	Auburn Hills, MI
lighting	**Stefan Graf, Illuminart**
	Mojtaba Navaab, University of Michigan
architect	**CRSS Architects, Inc.**
interior	**CRSS Architects, Inc.**
photographer	**Balthazar Korab**

The styling dome is designed to allow manufacturer's engineers to see prototypes under conditions that simulate daylight as much as possible. Sky conditions are simulated by concealed light sources in two accessible perimeter coves uplighting the dome's surface. The designers specified 85 14-inch-diameter holes in the ceiling for theatrical lighting. Dichroic filters allow the reduction of the color temperature in steps from 5600 degrees Kelvin to 3000 degrees Kelvin, as required.

For indirect lighting, luminaires, and lamps used include Elliptipar with GE 40-watt 3500 degrees Kelvin biax, 350-watt HIR T-3 quartz with glass color-correction filtered and 5600 degrees Kelvin metal halide lamps. Product lighting is provided using custom luminaires with Hi End Systems GE 1200-watt M.S.R.

s h o w r o o m s

a n d   d i s p l a y

s h o w r o o m s
a n d
d i s p l a y

project **Allrich Gallery**
San Francisco, CA
lighting **Becca Foster**
architect **Suzanne Parsons**
interior **Suzanne Parsons**
photographer **Ken Rice**

Easy to re-lamp and maintain, energy efficient, with a constant color temperature, and high rendering capability, 60-watt and 100-watt PAR 38 Hir flood lamps are excellent choices for lighting the back of the artwork. Low-voltage recessed adjustable fixtures were installed in the niches.

The Allrich Gallery
Celebrates
Twenty
Years

project **Allrich Gallery**
San Francisco, CA
lighting **Becca Foster**
architect **Suzanne Parsons**
interior **Suzanne Parsons**
photographer **Ken Rice**

The track lighting installed in rectilinear configurations on the ceiling integrates well with the architecture, and provides maximum lighting flexibility for constantly changing shows.

project **Bomani Gallery**
San Francisco, CA
lighting **Becca Foster**
architect **Suzanne Parsons**
interior **George De Witt**
photographer **Ken Rice**

A suspended wire system with artful fixtures was installed in the entryway skylight well to keep in pace with both the contemporary furniture and the art displayed. Stunning wall-mounted articulating task luminaires are installed both at the reception desk and the owner's private office.

project
San Francisco Mart
San Francisco, CA
lighting
Randall Whitehead
architect
Andrew Batey
interior
Andrew Batey
photographer
Donna Kempner

A slowly rotating color wheel
turns static nylon cord into a
fantasy fountain. The task for
the interior designer was to do
something creative with the nylon
fiber used to make carpeting,
so he created a fountain. Using
an ellipsoidal theatrical fixture
fitted with a rotating color wheel,
the lighting designer was able
to give the nylon sculpture an
illusion of movement.

85

project   **Japanese American**
             National Museum
             Los Angeles, CA
lighting   **Susan Huey and**
             Hiram Banks
interior   **Gene Takeshita**
photographer **Beatriz Coll,**
             Coll Photography

Custom low-voltage, cool-beam accent lighting, suspended from a pole-mounted cable lighting system, provides safe and soft lighting for this rare and fragile exhibit. Since this building is a historical landmark, designers were prohibited from adding new lighting on ceilings or walls, so electric power was brought up through the floor.

project   **Display Light, Carmel Valley, CA**
lighting   **Donald Maxcy**
interior   **Donald Maxcy**
photographer **Batista Moon Studio**

A suspended truss with PAR lamps provides accent and soft ambient light. The apparent source of template lighting is from the truss, but concealed higher is the gobo pattern in a theatrical luminaire. The sense of calm and quiet presence in this vignette evokes a contemplative response from viewers.

project	**San Francisco Mart**
	San Francisco, CA
lighting	**Randall Whitehead**
architect	**Andrew Batey**
interior	**Andrew Batey**
photographer	**Donna Kempner**

Fashioned by architect Andrew Batey, a "dungeon" created from styrofoam allows a tiny shaft of light to illuminate its inner sanctum, one of a series of display windows created in a collaboration between designers from various fields and lighting consultant Randall Whitehead. A low-voltage PAR 36 lamp projects the tight beam of illumination, as if an unseen window allows a sliver of light to fall on the sequestered carpet.

s h o w r o o m s
a n d   d i s p l a y

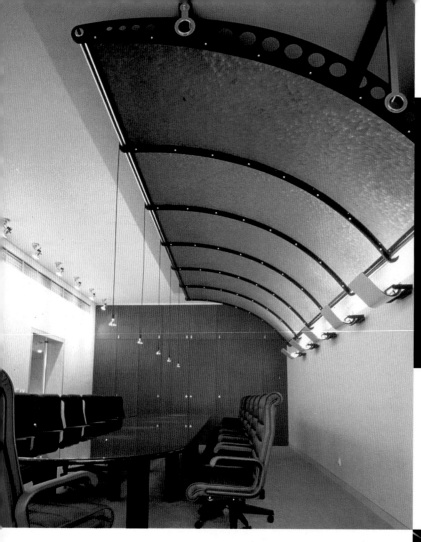

project
**Knoll International
GmbH Showroom
Frankfurt, Germany**
lighting
Lighting Design Partnership
interior architect
Studios Architecture
photographer
Engelhardt and Sellin

A rough screen of 40 cm by 40 cm spruce timbers, set like bridge trestles in a framework of vertical and standing uprights, runs across the back of the showroom.

project | **Toyota AMLUX Osaka
Osaka, Japan**
lighting | **Kaoru Mende**
architect | **Takenaka Corporation**
interior | **Fumio Enomoto,
Yasuo Kondo and
Daiko Corp.**
photographer | **Nacasa and Partners, Inc.**

This floor does double duty as a reception area, and is cross-illuminated by numerous recessed luminaires. The area lights from the ceiling, columns, and the wall in the back (wall washers on the aluminum wall), provide good overall illumination.

project | **Toyota AMLUX Osaka
Osaka, Japan**
lighting | **Kaoru Mende**
architect | **Takenaka Corporation**
interior | **Fumio Enomoto,
Yasuo Kondo and
Daiko Corp.**

photographer | **Nacasa and Partners, Inc.**

In the new Toyota AMLUX showroom in Osaka, the design of each floor from the first to the third is based on the concept of a building with circulating passages. A unique louvered ceiling under the deep eaves shines with soft, indirect light to impress visitors. Halogen lamps add sparkling effects, creating an even more dramatic welcome.

project
**United Chair Showroom
New York City, NY**
lighting
**Steven Bliss,
T. Kondos Associates**
interior
Tom Gass, Gass Design
photographer
Peter Paige

[right] Double-hung gathered sheers are illuminated by adjustable lamps suspended on cables from the slab above, and weighted by black spheres. The electrical cords hang loose and recess at the floor level through cutout mouse holes. This also allows air conditioning to flow from window wall to showroom. At full light level, the sheers become opaque; when dimmed, they become translucent and reveal the entire chair collection.

[bottom right] This conference table is lit by a recessed quarts floodlight installed in its base, which illuminates a suspended white disc overhead.

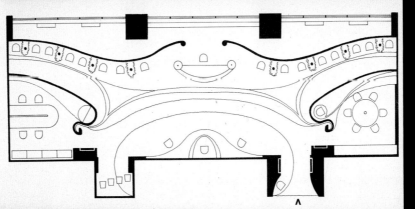

[diagram] Here, the lighting design challenge was to transform a nondescript, rectangular office space into a visually enticing contract chair showroom that would attract customers. In addition, the client needed areas to display a 30-product collection in its entirety, along with areas for reception, private conferences, work, and storage.

project **Amoco Fabric and Fibers Company Atlanta, GA**

lighting **Gandy/ Peace, Inc.**

interior **Gandy/ Peace, Inc.**

photographer **Chris A. Little**

The flexibility of Power trac lighting works well to enhance changing displays, and also illuminates movable Tiffany-style display windows.

project **Yarn Company Showroom Atlanta, GA**

lighting **Gandy / Peace, Inc.**

interior **Gandy / Peace, Inc.**

photographer **Chris A. Little**

[left] The drama created by this black space with its theatrical lighting caused record numbers of show attendees to stop and visit, thus introducing a new product to hundreds of people.

[below] The concept behind this 5,000-square-foot temporary showroom for a major yarn manufacturer was to provide a dramatic and simple space for seminars and cocktail parties, and to highlight and introduce new product information (coordinated with the overall advertising theme of "Leading the Revolution"). Simple, unobtrusive track lighting and "shop" fixtures provide flexible, economical, and effective fill and focus light.

showrooms and display

project   **Lackawana Leather Showroom**
               Chicago, IL
lighting   **Len Auerbach and Patricia Glasow**
architect   **Andrew Belschner and Joseph Vincent**
photographer   **Nick Merrick**

Custom adjustable armatures holding MR11 spot lamps graze the front of each hanging leather panel with light. Reflective metal squares on the floor, and mirrors on the wall behind the panels, scatter light around the room so additional fixtures are not needed to illuminate the back of the panels. Each leather panel is motorized to turn 360 degrees and is connected to a theatrical lighting control console, which programs the movement. Standard MR16 track fixtures with 50-watt flood lamps are used to illuminate the entry, leather drapery, and leather panel wall.

project   **Amoco Fabric**
               and Fibers Company
               Atlanta, GA
lighting   **Gandy/ Peace, Inc.**
interior   **Gandy/ Peace, Inc.**
photographer   **Chris A. Little**

The adjustable, low-voltage downlights in the vaulted ceiling provide quality lighting and contribute to the overall drama of this showroom. A dimmer system makes it easy to change the lighting for audio-visual presentations, which are essential program requirements of the showroom.

91

project
Conde House
San Francisco, CA
lighting
Alan and Joy Ohashi
architect
Alan and Joy Ohashi
interior
Alan and Joy Ohashi
photographer
Steve Burns

Because this space has a large amount of natural light, straightforward track lighting and low-voltage MR16 bulbs are all that is needed to provide sufficient illumination. Also, the showroom is designed to focus attention on furniture ensemble vignettes, so high keylights with alternating flood and spot bulbs to highlight specific areas work well with the vignette concept.

project   **Mottura Showroom**
             Los Angeles, CA
lighting   **Gensler and Associates**
architect   **Gensler and Associates**
interior   **Gensler and Associates**
photographer **Toshi Yoshimi**

The showroom functions not only as a display vehicle for merchandise, but also (according to the designers) as a three-dimensional statement of where retail is at, and where we think it is going. Adjustable track systems provide an economical way to vary lighting according to display needs for Mottura's evolving product lines.

project   **Klein Tools Showroom**
             Chicago, IL
lighting   **Gensler and Associates**
architect   **Gensler and Associates**
interior   **Gensler and Associates**
photographer **Marco Lorenzetti**

Two main areas under the modified roof provide a long, rectangular boardroom and a small museum, whose restricted light is appropriate for the display of memorabilia and tools in a series of special "jewel" cases.

project	Crystal Art
	Pleasanton, CA
lighting	Joel Miroglio
architect	Miroglio Architecture + Design
interior	Miroglio Architecture + Design
photographer	Alan Weintraub

A front view of the Crystal Art Store, showing custom display units illuminated by overhead low-voltage pendants that resemble sparkling crystals. Inside, custom display units are illuminated by recessed low-voltage spotlights overhead.

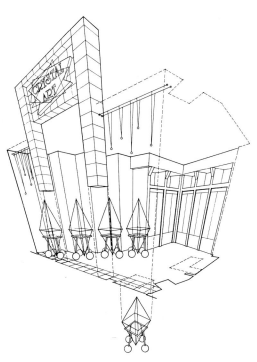

CRYSTAL ART

s h o w r o o m s
a n d   d i s p l a y

project	LaPorte's Fine Art
	Pacific Grove, CA
lighting	Linda Ferry
architect	Robert Jacoubowsky
interior	John Schneider
photographer	Greg Wutke

This gallery is a split-level space, with a combination of low and high ceilings. The entrance to the gallery is located two feet below street level, emphasizing the need for an inconspicuous lighting system. To minimize the visual impact of lighting equipment, recessed track with low-profile fixtures are employed in the lower ceiling. Track lighting is laid out in a rectangular shape to mirror the lines of the room, and to maximize lighting flexibility for changing exhibits. The track lighting is designed in sections, with sufficient loads to allow each piece of art to be spotlighted according to individual requirements.

project	**AMLUX: Toyota Auto Salone Tokyo Tokyo, Japan**
lighting	**TL Yamagiwa Laboratory**
architect	**Nikken Sekkei**
photographer	**Yamagiwa Corporation**

In this automobile showroom, the lighting concept is individualized for each type of car—sports, luxury, or off-road. The lighting effects for the sports car make it resemble a futuristic spaceship.

project	**Space Center Houston Houston, TX**
lighting	**Larry French**
architect	**Clive Grout**
interior	**Chuck Roberts and Bob Rogers**
photographer	**Paul Hester and Lisa Carol Hardaway**

The Apollo 17 spacecraft is mounted on a supporting frame over a shallow pit. A custom designed motion effect, created with compact fluorescent sources, is located inside the pit to add the ripple of expanding heat patterns to the heat shield. Static color, in oranges, yellows, and reds, to complement the motion effect, is made with standard fluorescent fixtures encased in ultraviolet-resistant and colored-tube sleeves. The pit itself is covered with a custom louver to shield the light source from view.

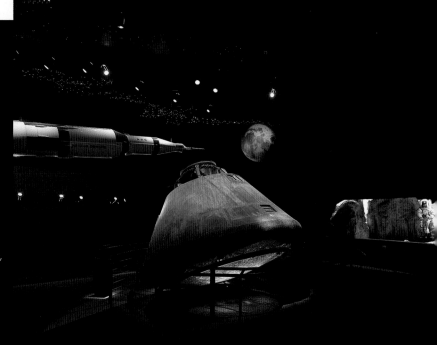

project	**The Dudley Perkins Harley-Davidson Showroom San Francisco, CA**
lighting	**Edward J. Cansino & Associates**
interior	**Christ Surunis, Davis Design Group; Brian O'Flynn, Murphy O'Flynn Design Associates**
photographer	**Douglas A. Salin**

Track lighting mounted on the concrete ceiling above the grid keeps the T-bar as uncluttered as possible. To downplay the morass of wire, pipe, and conduit running above, all elements at grid height and higher were painted black, effectively making these elements invisible. Though nearly 100 trackheads reside above the T-bar system, their black-painted components integrate seamlessly. Careful aiming and placement prevents glare from distracting customers.

project   **Expressions**
            Seattle, WA & Kirkland, WA
lighting   **Christopher Thompson,**
            David Story
photographer **David Story**

The lighting design provides a flexible and accessible lighting
system necessary for a showroom of this type.

BARS, CLUBS AND CAFES

intimate meeting places

Taverns, roadhouses, lounges, brew pubs, bars, and clubs—from ultra-classy to super funky—can take a dizzying variety of forms. Design is everything in these settings, as the mood is set by the surroundings. Happy, festive places evoke camaraderie. A quiet, sumptuous atmosphere creates a sense of intimacy and romance.

Lighting in bars and clubs can vary in the extreme.

Here, the designers can let their fantasy visions run wild, and the rules of lighting, such as foot candles and color temperature, become more flexible. No longer utilitarian, lighting in these settings becomes part of the pizazz.

In lighting bars and clubs, designers have discovered a myriad of non-traditional uses for traditional fixtures. Even the low-tech lava lamp finds new life as a design

component on huge outer-space-inspired luminaires. There is a great deal of freedom in creating designs for bars and clubs. Since each club vies with the next for patrons, the keynote of lighting clubs is drama. Functionality and flattering fill light take a back seat to mood lighting and flashy special effects. People long for an escape, even if it is just for a few hours. These

establishments can be a welcome oasis.

project
Mud Bug OTB
Chicago, IL
lighting
Aumiller Youngquist, P.C.
architect
Aumiller Youngquist, P.C.
interior
Aumiller Youngquist, P.C.
photographer
Tim Long Photography

A shot of the street elevation showing the cafe entry on the left and the old loading dock on the right. Blue neon letters highlight the no-nonsense exterior. The tower is visible from nearby North Avenue, a main thoroughfare.

project	**Mud Bug OTB**
	Chicago, IL
lighting	**Aumiller Youngquist, P.C.**
architect	**Aumiller Youngquist, P.C.**
interior	**Aumiller Youngquist, P.C.**
photographer	**Tim Long Photography**

A view of the main bar showing an artifact bartap and betting counters in the background. Abundant downlighting lets customers play without distraction.

project	Caroline's Comedy Club
	New York, NY
lighting	Paul Haigh
architect	Haigh.Architects.Designers
interior	Paul Haigh,
	Barbara H. Haigh
photographer	Elliot Kaufman

[above] The seating tiers of the club are accented with fiber optics and the "Caroline's" sign is highlighted with three-color bank lights.

[above] This detail view of the drinks rail at the rear of the theatre shows an uplight projection onto the concrete wall.

[below] This view of the free-standing bar tables, positioned below recessed downlights, shows the elliptical shape of the stone table tops projected onto the terrazzo floor.

Caroline's Comedy Nightclub New York City New York

When Caroline's Comedy Nightclub moved to Broadway in New York City and increased in size, the new space was totally revamped to match the style that owner Caroline Hirsch felt was required. The new space was huge and quite intimidating. The design objective was to create a club large enough to be profitable, but also to include more intimate areas where patrons could congregate in comfort.

Besides the main theater section, a bar area that also serves as a place for people to wait before shows was incorporated into the design.

Designers Paul and Barbara Haigh's aim was to fulfill these functions while retaining a sense of comfort in the vast space. They chose the atmosphere of a medieval fair as a theme for decor, using a harlequin pattern on birch plywood, velvets, and tapestries. Colorful banquettes provide some of the seating for the diners, and the harlequin pattern is carried throughout the club on tabletops, doors, the face of the bar, and carpets. Uplighting on the drink rails adds to the dazzling look.

Fiber optics outline various architectural features, to help patrons find their way through the club. Tiny incandescent lamps with shades dot the tables, creating inviting places to gather. Low-voltage, recessed, MR16 downlights highlight the bar tables, and recessed floor fixtures illuminate the wall and additional bar seating areas. Fiber-optic lights on the top of banquettes add color (two 150-watt metal halide illuminators use color wheels to vary the fiber optic lighting) and detail to the design. Velvet-paneled draperies, illuminated with the narrow spotlights of low-voltage, surface-mounted fixtures, help soften the feel of the space and allow different levels to be closed off, depending on crowd size.

Over the bar, half-inch fiber-optics on the soffit change color from magenta to aqua to green to white, with remote-controlled metal halide illuminators providing the main light source. Recessed fixtures with PAR36 narrow spots over fiber optics help light areas near the bar. These can be redirected as necessary.

For the theater, the unfinished concrete rear wall is uplit to highlight its unusual texture. Uplighting is also used to enhance tempered glass shelves along the bar's back wall. Lumiere outdoor fixtures, (they are actually swimming pool lights), recessed into the floor and lensed in different colors, cast interesting shadows on the walls, shelving, and drinks resting on the bar. Eleven banks of wall washers, housing nine 150-watt R40 lamps, each contain red, green, and blue lights that can be combined to make a variety of colors.

Caroline's is dramatic in more than just decor and lighting; the club is often used for television broadcasts. Because of this, versatility is built into the complex lighting systems of the space. A 48-patch Entertainer lighting console is preset to provide different backdrops for broadcasts. Architectural lighting uses a Versaplex system from Lutron.

From lounge to stairway to stage, Caroline's successfully integrates functional lighting design with a grand sense of theater.

project
**Caroline's Comedy Club
New York, NY**
lighting
Paul Haigh
architect
Haigh.Architects.Designers
interior
**Paul Haigh,
Barbara H. Haigh**
photographer
Elliot Kaufman

A detail view of main bar showing barfly stools. The glass soffit is downlit with recessed MR16 halogen lamps. The bar fascia is washed with light from fiberoptics. The back bar display is highlighted with recessed lights.

[inset] This view of the main bar/lounge shows the highlighted seating and dining areas. A curved architectural soffit is delineated with fiber-optic strings.

project
Velfarre
Tokyo, Japan
lighting
Stom Ushidate
architect
Robert R. Lowe
interior
Stom Ushidate
photographer
Nacasa & Partners Inc.

High-tech "monitor" wall sconces
and red spotlights set the mood in
this club lobby.

project
Velfarre
Tokyo, Japan
lighting
Stom Ushidate
architect
Robert R. Lowe
interior
Stom Ushidate
photographer
Nacasa & Partners Inc.

Custom-curved hood lights enhance the illusion of floating in space. The blue color of the hoods is highlighted with small aperture fixtures mounted in the ceiling.

**bars,
clubs,
and
cafes**

project
Velfarre
Tokyo, Japan
lighting
Stom Ushidate
architect
Robert R. Lowe
interior
Stom Ushidate
photographer
Nacasa & Partners Inc.

A spectacular shot of the reception area looking up from feature staircase. The designers used cracked glass and edge lighting to create an image of fantasy and the illusion of instability.

project **MG Planet**
         Tokyo, Japan
lighting **TL Yamagiwa Laboratory**
interior **Masanori Umeda**
photographer **Yoshio Shiratori**

A stainless-steel wire grid creates a boundary between the restaurant's actual space and the fantastical illusion of cosmic space expanding above the patrons. Thousands of miniature electric bulbs become a universe, thanks to mirrors on the surrounding walls.

bars,
clubs,
and
cafes

project **Yoshida Bar**
         Tokyo, Japan
lighting **Yukio Oka**
interior **Keizo Okazaki**
photographer **Atelier Fukumoto**

[above] Ambient lighting is provided by a sleek back-lit soffit, which gives the space a lush, comfortable atmosphere. Sandblasted glass bowls are suspended from the ceiling by nearly invisible stainless steel wire.

[left] Recessed downlights providing the illumination make these glass bowls seem to float on air, and cast diffused light over the bar counter. Glowing "brackets" appear to be helping hold up the ceiling with the strength of light itself.
To create a perfect balance, all of the lights are controlled by dimmers.

project	**MG Planet**	MG Planet attracts clientele from the fields of
	Tokyo, Japan	advertising and journalism. The "science fiction"
lighting	**TL Yamagiwa Laboratory**	atmosphere suggests that patrons are visiting
interior	**Masanori Umeda**	from other planets to enjoy "earth" food, music,
photographer	**Yoshio Shiratori**	and drinks.

project
America's Restaurant
Houston, TX
lighting
Jordan Mozer
architect
Larry Traxler
interior
Jordan Mozer
photographer
David Clifton

A pre-Columbian theme is carried
through the design of this
restaurant, from architecture to
artifacts. Here, the very walls
resemble woven cloth and the
pendants resemble some ancient
Mayan or Inca symbol. These
fantastic ceiling fixtures and wall
sconces are made of painted,
hand-cut aluminum and blown glass.

project
Surf 'n' Turf
Matsuyama, Japan
lighting
Jordan Mozer
architect
Jordan Mozer
interior
Jordan Mozer
photographer
Take Ichi

This dining area is lit by glowing
horns and sea-creature pendants.
The walls bulge, and even the
chairs join in the weird panorama.

project
Iridium
New York, NY
lighting
Jordan Mozer
architect
Jeff Carloss
interior
Jordan Mozer
photographer
Andrew Garn

For Iridium, the designers sought to infuse the space with the spirit of a dream or a poem: this nightspot is never what you expect, forms twist and curve in astonishing ways and the soft lighting brings out the startling effects.

project
Surf 'n' Turf
Matsuyama, Japan
lighting
Jordan Mozer
architect
Jordan Mozer
interior
Jordan Mozer
photographer
Take Ichi

Fantasy dream pendants, with glass tentacles as if from sea creatures, provide glowing, ambient light, and create a setting that surprises the senses.

project	**Stars California Restaurant**
	Frankfurt, Germany
lighting	**Jordan Mozer**
architect	**Jordan Mozer**
interior	**Jordan Mozer**
photographer	**Helmut Mitter**

Blown glass inserted into the tops of decorative columns conveys a feeling of pulsing matter and energy. Flowing star-like shapes on the wall add to the effect.

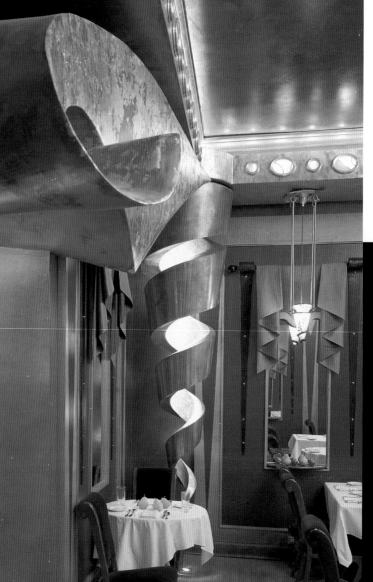

project
Vivere
Chicago, IL
lighting
Jordan Mozer
architect
Jordan Mozer
interior
Jordan Mozer
photographer
David Clifton

For Vivere, the designer looked to the spirals of Italian baroque architecture for inspiration. The tables are surrounded by spiral shapes, and a wall spiral is lit from within. Softly burnished gilt finishes reflect ambient light with an amber glow.

project **BACK LOT**
 of the After Dark
 Monterey, CA
lighting **Donald Maxcy**
architect **Donald Maxcy**
photographer **Russell Abraham**

Light draws the eye inside this sumptuous back bar. Mirrors enlarge the visual volume of the room and help bounce light around in the space. Chunks of glass block, glued together with silicone instead of mortar, are playfully reminiscent of ice cubes. The low-tech lights within the blocks are dimmable.

project **Harlands**
 Fresno, CA
lighting **Donald Maxcy**
architect **Kennedy Lutz**
 Architecture
interior **Charles Grebmeier**
photographer **Russell Abraham**

Lighting becomes artwork in this project. Subtle colored gels were used behind glass-block chair rails and block windows. A suspended low-voltage track system brings light down into the dining space and counter areas. The floating serpentine elements conceal lighting over the bar.

b a r s ,
c l u b s ,
a n d
c a f e s

project **The Sound Factory**
 San Francisco, CA
lighting **Terry Ohm**
photographer **Charles Cormany**

For the large dance room in this 20,000-square foot nightclub, 16 High End Systems Trackspots are suspended from a custom bracket, giving the illusion that the fixtures are floating in the air. A fully programmable robotic fixture, the Trackspot offers color changing, color mixing, movement, and pattern projection. The dance room also contains a Diversitronic strobe system, laser stimulators, and a fogger system.

THEATERS AND MOVIE HOUSES

s e t t i n g   t h e   m o o d

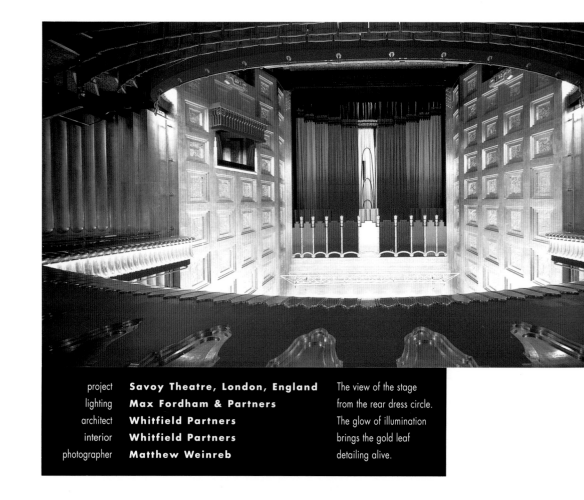

project	**Savoy Theatre, London, England**	The view of the stage
lighting	**Max Fordham & Partners**	from the rear dress circle.
architect	**Whitfield Partners**	The glow of illumination
interior	**Whitfield Partners**	brings the gold leaf
photographer	**Matthew Weinreb**	detailing alive.

Most of us thought that the dramatic, elegant movie palaces and theaters of the past were gone, with unimaginative multiplexes—no more than a series of boxes—left in their places. Well, what was lost is found again in a whole new generation of deluxe movie emporiums and dramatic theaters. Along with the newly-built are sumptuously remodeled and restored gems from our collective past.

Once again, the theater-going experience begins with the first glimpse of a brightly lit marquee, and continues into the lobby. The magic of movies and of live theater, much to the delight of the public, is spilling over into its environment. The best new lighting designs for theaters and movie houses enhance both restored period features and futuristic surfaces, lending a "larger than life" feeling to the interior surroundings.

Since the advent of video, which digs into movie revenues each time theater-goers choose to watch at home, the film industry has begun to take a hard look at where films are shown. To compete, the industry is striving to transform the movie-going experience back into something special. Lighting is an integral part of that change, and the new lighting methods work to create dynamic effects in the movie house, as well as on the movie screen.

project   **Savoy Theatre,**
            London, England
lighting   **Max Fordham & Partners**
architect   **Whitfield Partners**
interior   **Whitfield Partners**
photographer **Matthew Weinreb**

Viewed from the circle of the proscenium arch panel, stage
lighting within the coffer blends with the architecture.

project
**John L. Tishman
Auditorium
New School
for Social Research,
New York, NY**
lighting
Frank Kelly
architect
**Rolf Olhausen, Principal
Barbara Spandorf
Architects, Inc.**
interior
**Rolf Olhausen, Principal
Barbara Spandorf**
photographer
Brian Rose

Stage lighting was removed from the flanking arcades, which had never provided light from the proper angles. Some mounted fixtures were added on ladders at the back of the balcony, on either side of the projection booth. The most visible ones seem to slip discreetly from the shadows of one of the ceiling tiers; they can be lowered for maintenance and unplugged completely for events that call for showing the architectural purity of the space. Meanwhile, the arcades are free to celebrate themselves in the gleam of concealed downlights. A single control system operates architectural presets and a theatrical console.

John L. Tishman Auditorium New School for Social Research New York City New York

For many years, the lighting for the Tishman Auditorium at the New School for Social Research had provided both too much light and too little. Though the people on stage were overwhelmed by the glare, paradoxically, they still lacked good enough reading light for notes or scores. The subtle grays of the room had long given way to plain white. Much of the original design of the space had been changed, and its original atmosphere was totally lost.

Three years ago, the auditorium was restored to its original colors and given an expanded stage, refurbished furniture, and additional modern technical systems, as well as acoustical improvements. New lighting was designed as if the original architect, Joseph Urban, had been given access to today's technology when the auditorium was built in the thirties. Architect Rolf Ohlhausen, of Prentice and Chan, Olhausen Architects worked with lighting designer Frank Kelly, of Imero Fiorentino Associates, to restore the truly modern concept of the space.

Original cove lighting is retained in the upper tiers, but, for energy efficiency that does not sacrifice effect, halogen lamps replace standard incandescents. The intended gray shades of the interior are also restored, and benefit from the improved color rendering of the lighting. Permanent downlights on stage provide good reading light for performers. The overall stage lighting is greatly improved by the addition of QPAR 56 lights in concealed ceiling coves, ellipsoidal reflector spotlights on motorized lighting pipes flanking the stage, and ladder-mounted fixtures at the back of the balcony.

In the armrests of the seating, low-voltage strip lights illuminate the way for audience members. Above the doors, new soffits accommodate exit signs and emergency lighting.

General illumination is improved by recessed QPAR 56 adjustable downlights, which are adjacent to the original, luminous white glass panels that once provided most of the general light. A new, combination architectural/theatrical dimming system makes the auditorium more flexible with push-button preset stations for general classroom use and a memory console for theatrical performances.

In the lobby, the lighting is completely redone; recessed, compact fluorescent emergency lights replace one-by four-foot surface-mounted strips, and a flexible, compact fluorescent strip takes over for the ceiling cove's outmoded incandescent socket strips. Last, the new lighting's color temperature is 3500 degrees Kelvin carefully chosen to blend well with the abundant daylight spilling in through the auditorium's glass doors.

project
**John L. Tishman
Auditorium
New School for Social
Research, New York, NY**
lighting
Frank Kelly
architect
**Rolf Olhausen, Principal
Barbara Spandorf
Architects, Inc.**
interior
**Rolf Olhausen, Principal
Barbara Spandorf**
photographer
Brian Rose

In this auditorium's up-to-date lighting design, cove lighting repeats the flooring pattern in the lobby. Probably originally lit with strips of incandescents, the shapely cove recently sported surface-mounted fluorescent tubes before being restored to its intended color rendition with the use of compact fluorescents.

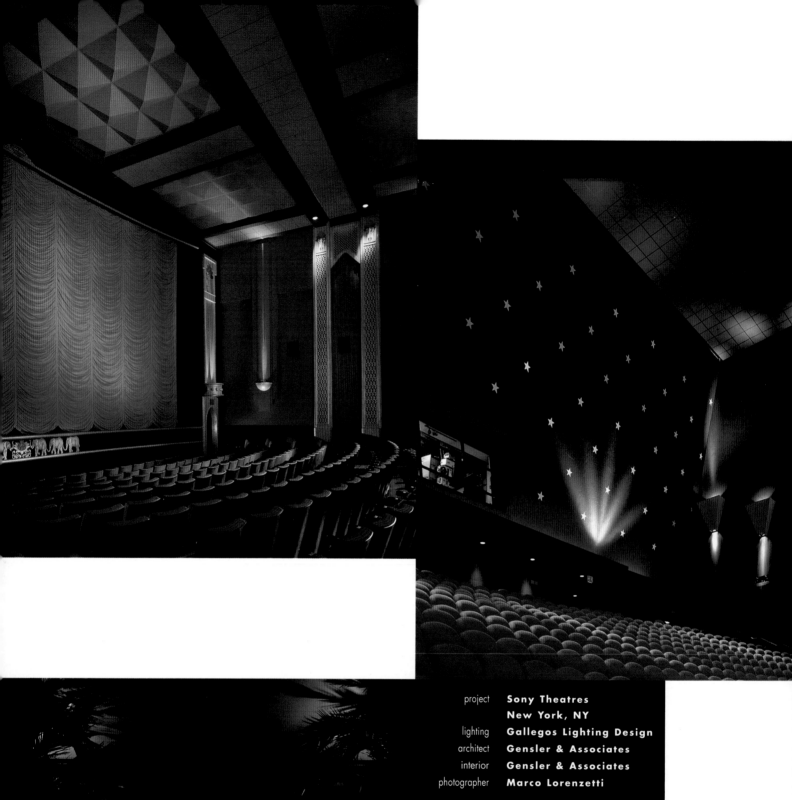

project   **Sony Theatres**
                New York, NY
lighting   **Gallegos Lighting Design**
architect   **Gensler & Associates**
interior   **Gensler & Associates**
photographer   **Marco Lorenzetti**

[above left] In the auditorium, wall sconces and
architectural details enhance the Art Deco flavor.
The indirect lighting is a refreshing change from the typical
sea of downlights so often seen in multiplexes of this type.

[above] Searchlights reach for the stars to create
an opening-night effect in the auditorium.

[left] In the main concessions hall, columns display
timelines of the history of film development. A grove of
ebony palms holds monitors that display current and
future attractions.

project	**Princess of Wales Theater**
	Ontario, Canada
lighting	**Wallace G. Eley**
	and D.R. Waite
architect	**Peter Smith**
interior	**George Yabu**
photographer	**Robert Burley**

To illuminate a painting by Stella, this system of 3500 degrees Kelvin, white triphosphor, cold-cathode tubing in a preformed dome was chosen for its excellent color-rendering properties and dimming flexibility. For aesthetic effect and definition, a line of clear lamps, dimmed to 50 percent for long life, is installed to form a trapezoidal ring at the base of the dome. This also makes maintenance easy. The upper part of the dome is surrounded with a series of PAR 20 halogen lamps.

project
Princess of Wales Theater
Ontario, Canada
lighting
Wallace G. Eley and D.R. Waite
architect
Peter Smith
interior
George Yabu
photographer
Robert Burley

A system of coves with 60-watt A lamps on
16-inch centers over the balcony, dress circle, and
orchestra level seating was installed to provide the
indirect lighting.

project	**Fitzgerald Theater, St. Paul, MN**
lighting	**Duane Schuler**
architect	**Miller Hanson Westerbeck Berger, Inc.**
photographer	**George Heinrich**

Custom decorative sconces, with dimmed incandescent lamps, were added
to this auditorium's side walls at all balcony and box levels. Downlights are
placed in the ceiling at locations that allow them to be re-lamped from above
via catwalks. On the stage, a new orchestra shell contains downlights
with halogen PAR 64 lamps to provide approximately 80 foot-candles of
illumination. In addition, new theatrical lighting locations were added to the
audience boxes and on the faces of the balconies.

theaters
and movie
houses

project **Sony Theatres**
New York, NY
lighting **Gallegos Lighting Design**
architect **Gensler & Associates**
interior **Gensler & Associates**
photographer **Marco Lorenzetti**

[right] This wonderful mural is a collage of the great entry marquees from Sony Theaters. The excitement of the space is enhanced by the sweeping city views, the movement of multiple escalators, and the colorful drama of the artwork. The mural is illuminated using theater luminaires mounted near the top of the columns.

[below] Sony Pictures Entertainment's new complex near Lincoln Center is the flagship for its cinema operations, as well as its premiere theater. The dynamic entry uses richly colored signage and interior lighting to create an enticing look.

[below right] This concessions stand entrance is a replica of the entry gate at Sony's main lot in Culver City, California. While recalling the past, the stand incorporates lush, modern bands of neon color overhead.

theaters and movie houses

project	**Glyndebourne Opera House
Lewes, East Sussex, England**
lighting	**George Sexton**
architect	**Michael Hopkins,
Patty Hopkins and Robin Snell**
photographer	**Richard Davies**

Custom, curved architectural slots at the perimeter walls house an incandescent strip light system, which washes the wood paneling and gives the theatre a stunning glow. Shallow concrete coffers are fitted with miniature incandescent light sources to provide a halo of ambient light. A series of miniature downlights, integrated into the modulating ceiling bands, cast a glow of light onto the seats and add to the "sky of stars" seen across the theatre. In addition, theatrical PAR 56 fixtures suspended from the central lighting bridge, highlight the balconies.

project	**Sendai Shi Bunka Center
Tokyo, Japan**
lighting	**TL Yamagiwa Laboratory**
architect	**Yamashita Sekkej Inc.**
photographer	**Yamagiwa Corporation**

The stage of this concert hall is illuminated with recessed downlight fixtures and recessed lights diffused by glittering light reflectors. The suspended sound reflector is height-adjustable to fit each program, its sparkling look is created by a downlight in the ceiling.

theaters and movie houses

project	**Seafort Square Theater
Tokyo, Japan**
lighting	**Shunji Tamai**
architect	**RIA Company, Ltd.**
interior	**RIA Company, Ltd.**
photographer	**Courtesy of Shunji Tamai**

This side view of the auditorium shows the custom-mounted luminaires. Recessed fixtures provide additional light.

project	**Skylight Opera Theater**	The lighting design for the auditorium combines exposed lamp sources and hidden sources to enhance
	Milwaukee, WI	the theatrical painting and provide an inviting atmosphere for patrons. The central chandelier and the
lighting	**Robert Shook and Duane Schuler**	sconces at the gallery faces provide the focal points of light. Recessed downlights in the galleries and
architect	**Sherrill Myers**	uplights onto the ceiling reveal the painted surfaces. All sources are dimmed incandescent, to meet the
interior	**David Birn and David Zinn**	criteria for opera performances and to increase lamp life. Theatrical lighting for the stage is integrated
photographer	**Mark Gubin**	into the box openings near the stage, on railings at the gallery faces, and at a fourth-floor technical
		gallery, painted to resemble the seating galleries below.

117

project
Private Theater
architect
**Backen Arrigoni and
Ross Architects**
photographer
Douglas A. Salin

This lush setting for private viewings
has all the advantages of a large-scale
theater, with the intimacy of a more
compact setting. Low-profile recessed
lighting brings up the sheen of
upholstery. A well-planned dimming
system allows for a classroom setting,
as well as comfortable movie-watching.

project
**Boehringer Ingelheim
Pharmaceuticals
Richfield, CT**
lighting
Childs & Scolze
architect
Gensler & Associates
interior
Gensler & Associates
photographer
Marco Lorenzetti

Wall-washing light adds drama to a
grid-patterned wall.

project   **Yerba Buena Gardens
              Visual Arts Center
              San Francisco, CA**
lighting   **Patricia Glasow, Len Auerbach,
              Principal Mark Rudiqer**
architect   **Maki and Associates
              Robinson, Mills + Williams**
photographer **John Barnes Photography**

The Forum, a flexible theatrical
space, incorporates three
complete lighting systems:
theatrical performance lighting,
tungsten halogen downlighting
for performances and parties,
and metal halide downlighting
for brightly lit activities.

project
**Alcazar Theater
San Francisco, CA**
interior lighting
David Ebert
exterior lighting
Teal Brogden
architect
Bill Pearson
interior
David Ebert
photographer
Robert Swanson

[left] The style of this eclectic building is Moorish and Byzantine. The exterior materials are glazed terra cotta tile, and brick, with marble panels at the entrance, and recessed stucco walls. Strategically placed uplighting throws fanciful architectural detail into theatrical relief.

[below left] Original interior embellishment of the theater is modest, limited to the main entrance and assembly areas. Cove lighting in the entryway creates an enticing air of mystery. Deeply recessed "star" windows, illuminated from within, cast dramatic, sculptural shadows.

OFFICE SPACES

hospitable work environments

chapter eight

Office environments are reaching new levels of comfort. Today, the cold, almost clinical spaces of traditional office design have given way to a more residential style. A greater use of texture and color by interior designers and architects is being combined with a new approach to corporate lighting. Standard office lighting design once consisted of two- by four-foot recessed fluorescent fixtures suspended in a ceiling grid. This made

for a work environment filled with a harsh, somewhat depressing light. The first step toward changing this practice came with the introduction of indirect light sources that bounced light off the ceiling to create a soft overall glow. Since this method, by itself, still looks flat, decorative fixtures and accent lights are now added to provide visual

interest and sparkle.

The color quality of fluorescents and high-intensity discharge sources has also improved. In addition, ultra-quiet, solid-state ballasts and very compact light sources allow for a much more friendly use of energy-efficient lamps. In planning office lighting schemes, the challenge is to be creative

and energy-concious at the same time. The realities of energy regulations do not have to dampen the spirit of good design: many of the projects featured in this chapter don't resemble traditional offices at all. Their success demonstrates how greatly office spaces have changed for the better in just the last few years.

project	**The Port of Oakland Oakland, CA**	The expansive wood conference table provides a warm visual anchor to this
lighting	**Horton Lees Lighting**	voluminous conference room. Recessed low-
architect	**Robinson Mills + Williams**	voltage downlights enhance the color of the
interior	**Robinson Mills + Williams**	table while clean-lined wall sconces bounce
photographer	**Bob Swanson**	amber light off the barrel-vault ceiling.

project	**Epic Records**
	Santa Monica, CA
lighting	**Cosimo Pizzulli**
architect	**Cosimo Pizzulli**
interior	**Cosimo Pizzulli**
photographer	**Fashid Assassi**

Suspended "floating cloud" ceilings cover approximately
51 percent of this open area with 1.5-inch-thick fiberglass.
The fiberglass material helps reflect ambient lighting within
open workstations.

Gore-Tex
Japan
Setagaya
Tokyo

Gore-Tex, a famous manufacturer of synthetic fiber products, uses "Be Creative" as a corporate motto. Interior designer Masanori Umeda, along with lighting design by Ushiospax, sought to meet that challenge. They created an exciting design that makes the Gore-Tex space much more than an ordinary office environment, and conveys a feeling of the great outdoors.

The entrance hall features a huge, fiber-optic world map. Indirect ambient light comes from compact metal halide lamps reflecting light off the ceiling. The walls on the first floor are aluminum, silk-screened with a pattern of Gore-Tex fiber. The lighting design purposely keeps the office entrance very bright during daylight hours, with diminishing lighting as one progresses through the building, to give the eyes a chance to adjust naturally from daylight to interior light.

The lobby and meeting area evoke the panorama of the Mongolian plains, with

cloud-like sculptural forms hanging over the area. Luminaires, using halogen lamps, filtered through blue films and prisms, provide the overall punch light.
A circular screen of a lightly finished polycarbonate hints at the shape of a Pao, the Mongolian moveable house.

In the lounge, round anodized titanium bars reflect rainbow colors to create a wonderful screen. The bar counter is constructed of

natural materials, making a forest-like setting for eating and drinking. Accent lights tucked between the ceiling beams highlight the table tops and bar surface. Mini-halogen lamps mounted on the stool legs light up the circular base panels.

This delightful combination of varied lighting, wood finishes, and imaginatively colored metals brings a needed warmth to the interiors of this large corporation.

project
**Gore-Tex Japan
Setagaya, Tokyo**
lighting
Ushiospax
architect
Sato Kogyo
interior
Masanori Umeda
photographer
Yoshio Shiratori

On the wall by the reception counter, a world map indicates the locations of Gore-Tex branches with red, fiber-optic lights. Basic lighting is indirect but bright, using compact metal halide sources. The walls at the ground floor are aluminum, silk screened with the pattern of Gore-Tex fiber.

project
**Gore-Tex Japan
Setagaya, Tokyo**
lighting
Ushiospax
architect
Sato Kogyo
interior
Masanori Umeda
photographer
Yoshio Shiratori

[top]
The titanium bar area is anodized to show beautiful rainbow colors, and emphasized with halogen spotlights. The intended effect is that of a forest glade.

[bottom]
This space is designed to evoke the Mongolian plains. Below the ceiling, cut-outs represent a sea of clouds. Accent lights fitted with blue filters and prisms help punctuate the space. The circular screen is made of polycarbonate and hints at the image of a Pao, the Mongolian movable house.

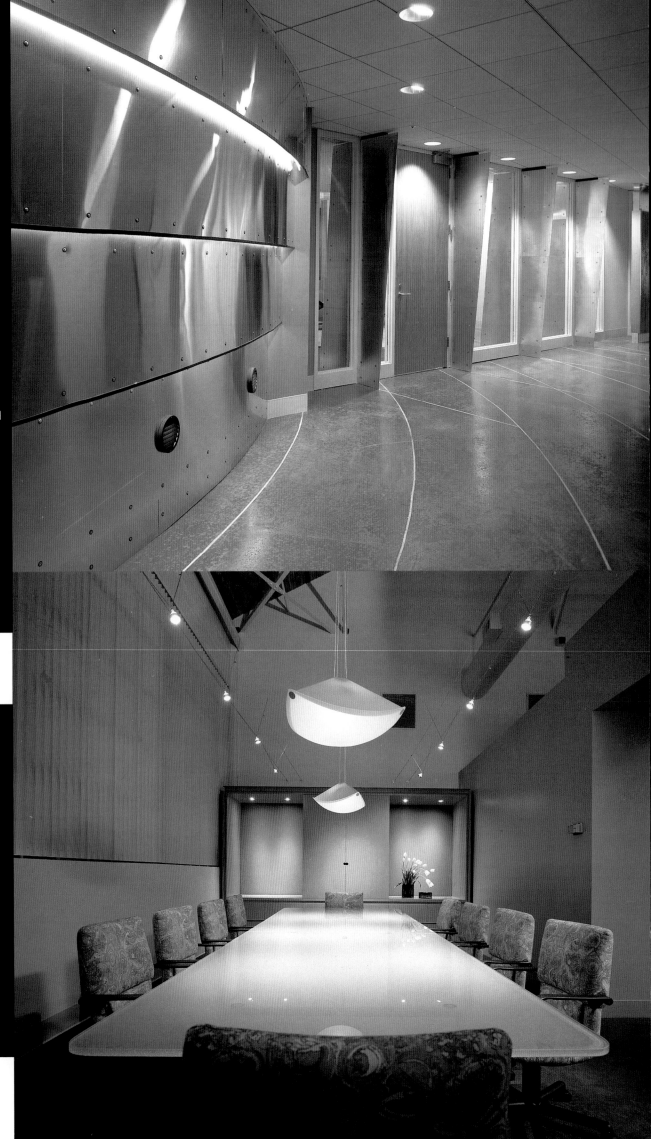

project
**AT&T Bay Area
Special Services
Center
Oakland, CA**
lighting
**Randall Whitehead
and Catherine Ng**
architect
**John Lum,
Mike Beam, Reid &
Tarics Associates**
interior
**John Lum,
Mike Beam, Reid &
Tarics Associates**
photographer
Christopher Irion

The plans for AT&T's Bay Area
Special Services Center called for
a playful space. Saddled with the
tight wattage constrictions of
California's Title 24 energy code,
the lighting design team employed
fluorescent and high-intensity
discharge sources in creative
ways. At the entryway, workers
and visitors are greeted by a
huge cantilevered steel wall.
This imposing facade is lit from
beneath with a rosy pink neon,
which reflects off the terrazzo
floor. Lensed fluorescent wall
washers cast a similar hue on
wedge-shaped wing walls.

project
**Jack Morton
Productions
San Francisco, CA**
lighting
Susan Huey, LIT
architect
Interior Architects
interior
Interior Architects
photographer
Beatriz Coll

To maintain the open ceiling and
exposed truss architecture, the
lighting design team specified a
suspended cable-lighting system
to provide ambient light for the
table and presentation wall.

project	**Apple Computer, Inc.**
	Research and Development Campus
	Building 2
	Cupertino, CA
lighting	**S. Leonard Aurbach Associates**
architect	**HOK**
interior architect	**Studios Architecture**
photographer	**Mark Darley**

The user groups in Building Two work building-wide, but are distributed locally into workteams. They requested large central "User Defined Areas," so that members of each group would run across colleagues working far away. Frosted glass walls allow light to be shared between spaces. Whimsical pendants provide abundant light with a playful touch.

office spaces

project **Latham & Watkins**
San Francisco, CA
lighting **S. Leonard Auerbach**
& Associates
architect **Babey Moulton, Inc.**
interior **Babey Moulton, Inc.**
photographer **Nick Merrick**

The gallery and pre-function conference zone of this office has abundant daylight at the two narrow ends of a rectangular space. The natural light is balanced with recessed incandescent downlights and wall washers, to highlight a collection of photographs.

o f f i c e
s p a c e s

project **Young & Rubicam**
San Francisco, CA
lighting **Richard Hannum**
architect **Hannum Associates**
interior **Richard Hannum**
photographer **Christopher Irion**

In this law office, a barrel vault is illuminated with twin light strips recessed into a cove. Arches are backlighted with 60-watt lamps mounted behind custom, perforated metal screen walls. Low-voltage recessed adjustable MR16 downlights add additional illumination.

project **Bank of America**
San Francisco, CA
lighting **Hiram Banks, LIT**
architect **Interior Architects**
interior **Interior Architects**
photographer **Beatriz Coll**

Specially mounted low-voltage track fixtures highlight the artwork, while staggered trimline fluorescent fixtures, concealed within the architecture, provide ambient illumination.

project
The Estate of James Campbell
Oahu, Hawaii
lighting
Susan Huey and Hiram Banks
interior architect
Ferraro Choi and Associates, Ltd.
photographer
Jon Miller

Layers of fluorescent indirect lighting, low-voltage
task illumination, and focus lighting are combined
with palm-leaf light patterns projected on textured
walls to illuminate this corporate lobby.

project   **The Estate of James Campbell**
                  Oahu, Hawaii
lighting   **Susan Huey and Hiram Banks**
interior architect   **Ferraro Choi & Associates, Ltd.**
interior   **Ferraro Choi and Associates, Ltd.**
photographer   **Jon Miller**

Cobalt-blue ambient lighting complements the red LED and VDT displays of this computer center. At the touch of a button, the blue light transforms into white light for system maintenance.

project
Oracle Corporation
lighting
**James Benya,
Luminae Souter
Lighting Design**
architect
**Ehrlich Rominger
Architects**
interior
Laura Seccombe
photographer
Douglas A. Salin

The Oracle Company is a database software company located in Silicon Valley. The playful theme of the employee lunchroom gives some welcome relief from the intense work situation. The cold cathode and neon colors blend together to create a lavender glow, while the art and wall panels are punched up with a low-voltage track system using miniature mirror reflector lamps. The pendant fixtures along the back provide a sense of separation for the banquet seating.

project   **Sony Music Entertainment
London, UK**
lighting   **Harper Mackay Ltd.**
architect   **Harper Mackay Ltd.**
interior   **Harper Mackay Ltd.**
photographer   **Dennis Gilbert**

The high-tech look of this office cafeteria is enhanced with "floating" light planes that provide light without overpowering the space.

project
**ZD Labs, A division of
Ziff Davis Publishing
Sunnyvale, CA**
lighting
**Thomas J. Skradski,
Luminae Souter
Lighting Design**
architect
**Gene Conti and
Michael Ott**
interior
**Gene Conti and
Michael Ott**
photographer
John Sutton

This equipment testing lab required
low-level, non-glare illumination for the
technicians. The solution is a combination
of indirect wall sconces, which provide
drama and open up the dark ceiling cavity,
supported by fiber-optic tubing that outlines
the equipment racks to create a sense
of electricity. Color also plays a key role
in visually enhancing this public showcase.
In addition, louvered track lighting is used
for task light.

project
**Sony Pictures Entertainment
Los Angeles, CA**
lighting
Joe Kaplan Lighting Design
architect
Gensler & Associates
interior
Gensler & Associates
photographer
Marco Lorenzetti

Sony Theatre's new office complex near Lincoln Center serves as both the company's flagship facility, and a premiere theater. This dynamic entry incorporates an elaborate marquee and interior lighting to create an enticing look.

project	**New York State Education Building, Albany, NY**
lighting	**Bill Lam, Bob Osten and Paul Zaferiou**
architect	**Einhorn Yaffee Prescott**
interior	**Einhorn Yaffee Prescott**
photographer	**Jeff Goldberg**

These new compact fluorescent sconces mark major circulation paths and identify destinations, such as the main reception desk. Here, visible luminaires are limited to the newly constructed architectural element, which floats within the original spaces. Fluorescent uplighting concealed in the top of this element provides a soft, cheerful rendering of the vaulted shapes above. Over the original daylights, concealed metal halide downlighting supplements daylight and provides a nighttime ambient glow.

project
**Sony Music Publishing
Conference Room
Santa Monica, CA**
lighting
Cosimo Pizzulli
architect
Cosimo Pizzulli
interior
Cosimo Pizzulli
photographer
Fashid Assassi

This conference room incorporates
state-of-the-art audio-visual and
televideo conferencing controls in
the custom designed tables and
cabinetry. A CAD system was used
to plan and develop area coverage
for the acoustical system and
task/ambient lighting system.

project	**Babcock & Brown**
	San Francisco, CA
lighting	**Thomas J. Skradski,**
	Luminae Souter
architect	**Studios Architecture**
interior	**Studios Architecture**
photographer	**Paul Warchol**

The conference room is lit with a louvered low-voltage
cable system, which appears to float in front of the
panoramic view. Asymmetrical T8 fluorescent signlighters
with electronic ballasts wash the presentation walls.
The frosted-glass table top glows from louvered PAR30
halogen uplights bolted to the floor. MR16 luminaires highlight a sculptural column, enhancing its spectacular finish.

project	**The Offices of**
	Plunkett Raysich
	Milwaukee, WI
lighting	**Steven Klein,**
	Principal;
	Lana Nathe
architect	**Stephen Holzhaver**
interior	**Nancy Arriano**
photographer	**Mark Heffron**

Basic geometric shapes are the design motif of
the pendants in the main conference room.
The presentation board wall is defined by cone
aperture wallwashers with MR16 lamps.

project
Sedgwick James & Company
San Francisco, CA
lighting
Horton Lees Lighting Design
architect
Christopher Pollock, Kei Yamagami, Gensler & Associates
interior
Gensler & Associates
photographer
Marco Lorenzetti

A four-floor interconnecting stair located at the elevator contains fluorescent cove lighting, which punctuates landings and enhances a sculptural railing design. Ambient lighting is used throughout the office to provide a high-quality environment suitable for VDT use.

project
McKenna, Conner & Cuneo
Los Angeles, CA
lighting
Patrick Quigley & Associates
architect
Gensler & Associates
interior
Gensler & Associates
photographer
Toshi Yoshimi

Curved walls articulated in wood paneling create interest and relief from the square format of the building. They are detailed with a black reveal and small, square, flush-mounted light fixtures, both of which suggest an illuminated two-dimensional arcade. The doors to the attorneys' offices have frosted-glass inserts, allowing light to filter into the secretarial space while assuring privacy for the attorneys.

project   **Talingent Corporation**
              Cupertino, CA
lighting   **Studios Architecture**
interior   **Studios Architecture**
photographer   **Sharon Risedorph**

The community areas were created to reinforce Talingent's culture and to provide as much interaction as possible between the engineers.

project
Enron Corp.
Houston, TX
lighting
Theo Kondos
Associates
architect
Gensler & Associates
interior
Gensler & Associates
photographer
Nick Merrick

"The Energizer": The name itself
suggests energy, vitality, and
animation, the ambiance Enron
desired for its employee cafeteria.
Visitors to this corporate dining
facility are greeted by a dramatic
graphic display. Created through
projected light, this graphic image
tumbles along the entry corridor
leading visitors into the dining area.

project
Taylor Smith
Houston, TX
lighting
Gensler & Associates
architect
Gensler & Associates
interior
Gensler & Associates
photographer
Nash Baker

Seeking to provide innovative and
inexpensive lighting throughout this
office, the lighting design team hit
upon a source of functioning light
fixtures in buildings that were slated
for demolition. These fixtures were
re-lamped, cleaned, and installed
as the major source of office
lighting. Three-wire industrial lights
were clamped to existing ceiling
tees, plugged into a duplex outlet,
and mounted to the ceiling grid.

project
Babcock & Brown
San Francisco, CA
lighting
Thomas J. Skradski,
Luminae Souter
Lighting Design
architect
Studios Architecture
interior
Studios Architecture
photographer
Paul Warchol

[left] Custom low-voltage fixtures with lockable aiming positions on a cable system provide indirect and accent light, and reflect in the perforated metal "wing" over the reception area and through the conference room. For ease of maintenance and good color rendering, the custom wall sconces use double-envelope halogen lamps for indirect illumination and the frosted glass is edge-lit with low-voltage xenon frosted lamps.

o f f i c e

s p a c e s

project
Russ Building
San Francisco, CA
lighting
Thomas J. Skradski,
Luminae Souter
Lighting Design
renovation architect
Laurie Petipas
photographer
Douglas A. Salin

[right] Each of the three main elevator lobbies in this office has a Gothic chandelier, quartz incandescent sconces above the elevators, and an elevator sign. The lighting designers had the chandeliers removed, cleaned, rewired and refitted with 13- and 39-watt compact fluorescent lamps at 2700 degrees Kelvin for energy efficiency. Similarly, the formerly incandescent elevator signs were removed, cleaned, and rewired with 9-watt compact fluorescent lamps. At the end of hall, a wall is made into a focal point with light from quartz wallwashers highlighting a mounted period tapestry. Quartz PAR 38 accent lights shine on the floor, plants, and stairs.

ELEVATORS.
TOPS 17 TO 30 FLOOR

project
Parsons Brinckerhoff
New York, NY
lighting
William Whistler, Brennan Beer
Monk / Interiors; Kristina Selles,
Wheel Gersztoff Shankar Selles Inc.
architect
Jo Anna Becker, Brennan Beer
Monk / Interiors
interior
William Whistler, Regula Onstad,
Brennan Beer Monk / Interiors
photographer
Peter Paige

[left] Parsons Brinckerhoff's boardroom responds to the growing communications needs of a firm on the cutting edge of technology. Concealed behind grid-patterned bronze doors, there is a high-tech video screen with rear projection, capable of receiving and transmitting images from any computer within the firm's worldwide network. In addition, two electronic white boards are also computerized for the reproduction of hard copy images of whatever is drawn on their surface.

project   **Doctors Company,**
Napa, CA
lighting   **Thomas J. Stradski,**
Stephanie B. Cissna, Luminae
Souter Lighting Design
lighting fixture designer
Christina Spann / Lightspann
architect   **Hill Architects**
interior   **Richard Pollack Associates**
photographer   **John Sutton**

[right] Elegant custom pendants and wall sconces with energy-efficient compact fluorescent lamps provide soft ambient illumination in the second-floor reception area. Dichroic glass medallion details on wall sconces can be viewed from above. The openings are fitted with soft white acrylic diffusers. Small-aperture MR16 adjustable accent lights enhance colors and reveal textures.

project   **One Lafayette Centre**
Washington D.C.
lighting   **William Whistler,**
Brennan Beer Gorman Monk / Interiors;
George Sexton III,
George Sexton Associates
architect   **Brennan Beer Gorman / Architects**
interior   **William Whistler,**
Brennan Beer Gorman Monk / Interiors
photographer   **Maxwell MacKenzie**

[below] Custom bronze lighting fixtures incorporated into the concierge desks complement the wall and ceiling light design. The ceiling lights required low-profile fixtures set within a decorative stained wood and bronze latticework.

project
Rosenberg Management
Orinda, CA
lighting
Randall Whitehead
and Catherine Ng
architect
Reid & Tarics Associates
interior
Mike Beam
photographer
Christopher Irion

[below] Indirect peach-hued fluorescent lamps cast a warm glow of illumination into this conference room. The main goal of the design is to blend the lighting elements into the architecture. Certain areas, including this conference room, have sheetrock ceilings instead of the typical T-Bar grid with acoustical tiles. This gives a more solid feeling to the space and allows for the introduction of vaulted ceiling details. The indirect lighting helps emphasize the coving, while creating an inviting fill light. At the apex of the vault, a series of slots house small, recessed adjustable low-voltage fixtures. These luminaires give the room visual punch.

project	**Gunne Sax Clothing**
	Corporate Offices
	San Francisco, CA
lighting	**Architectural Lighting Design**
architect	**Hanns Kainz & Associates**
interior	**Hanns Kainz & Associates**
photographer	**Douglas A. Salin**

The building, housing the corporate offices for this upscale manufacturer of women's and children's clothing, makes a dynamic visual statement. The designers combined a generous amount of daylight with cool colors to create a crisp, refreshing impression. Simple fluorescent strip fixtures were fitted with blue lamp sleeves to create a neon look for a fraction of the cost. Incandescent downlights warm up the pathway leading to the upper and lower floors.

[diagram, Herald Square Building]

The pylons contain two lamps (plan, top), one of which illuminates the top of the fixture. Beams from a lower lamp (sections, left) bounce off a mirror into the tube and are diffused by a sheet of optical film that lines the shaft. A second reflective film, which is adhered to the first, controls the amount of light exiting the tube; more rays are allowed to escape from the bottom to compensate for the greater light intensity near the source at the top. A mirror-like film at the end of the tube reflects light back into the housing.

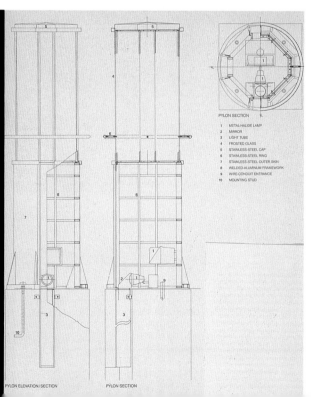

PYLON SECTION

1   METAL-HALIDE LAMP
2   MIRROR
3   LIGHT TUBE
4   FROSTED GLASS
5   STAINLESS-STEEL CAP
6   STAINLESS-STEEL RING
7   STAINLESS-STEEL OUTER SKIN
8   WELDED-ALUMINUM FRAMEWORK
9   WIRE-CONDUIT ENTRANCE
10 MOUNTING STUD

PYLON ELEVATION/SECTION   PYLON SECTION

project
Herald Square Building
Washington, D.C.
lighting
Yann Leroy, Brennan Beer
Gorman / Architects
architect
Peter Gorman, Brennan Beer
Gorman / Architects
interior
Jo Anna Becker, Brennan Beer
Gorman / Architects
photographer
Maxwell MacKenzie

The building's crown is highlighted by ten lighting pylons of stainless steel and frosted glass, measuring 12 inches high by 42 inches wide. The octagonal fixtures are fitted with metal halides for maximum light generation and are anchored to the granite facade at the ninth-story setback. The overall effect is that of a medieval structure or sculpted industrial machine. The lighting is duplicated at half their width and at the height of the retail base. Fluorescent sources provide the street-level lighting.

MEDICAL CARE FACILITIES

comfort the first priority

In medical care facilities, special attention must be paid to illumination, because older or unwell people are more sensitive to lighting levels and sources. Lighting must be glare free and very unobtrusive, yet must offer plenty of task illumination for medical care personnel.

Good ambient illumination is the first step; providing the necessary soft fill light to make rooms comfortable, and to help lessen any disorientation that patients may experience.

Task light must also be especially well-thought-out, since medical personnel often have urgent duties and little time to set up a sufficient light source. Patients or residents require especially good lighting in areas such as bathrooms, as their visual acuity may be impaired. As in other public spaces, accent light should be used to lead people to specific destinations—such as reception, admissions, and waiting rooms, or to help to direct people away from private or restricted areas.

Good design, with well-integrated lighting, goes a long way toward making a stay in a health care facility more pleasant. The effect of environment on health is well-known, so the designer's goal is to make the setting therapeutic, rather than stressful. To that end, the projects that follow may astound you. Never before has "light as art" become one of the healing arts.

project
**Health Park Medical Center
Lee County, FL**
lighting
Craig Roeder
architect
HKS Inc., Architects
interior
**HKS Designcare /
Medical Space Design**
photographer
Robt. Ames Cook

Theatrical metal halide fixtures, fitted with dichroic filters, project a fanciful rainbow of color on the curvilinear balconies.

project
**Health Park Medical Center
Lee County, FL**
lighting
Craig Roeder
architect
HKS Inc., Architects
interior
**HKS Designcare /
Medical Space Design**
photographer
Robt. Ames Cook

The atrium of the Health Park Hospital is washed with rainbows of light from metal-halide lamps with dichroic color filters.

Le Bonheur Children's Medical Center Memphis Tennessee

People who are ill or injured deserve to be surrounded by comfort and beauty. Until recently, neither hospital administrators nor hospital architects and designers gave much weight to the role of the environment in a patient's recovery. "Institutional" was the word of the day, and design formulas for such locations led to efficient, sterile, dully uniform surroundings. These days, however, competition is forcing hospitals to create friendlier spaces, to attract patients to their facilities. Designers are now able to create dramatic centers of warmth and beauty, enhanced through lighting.

Le Bonheur Children's Medical Center in Memphis exemplifies the new trend in hospital and medical facilities. Lighting designer Craig Roeder, given free rein to create beauty and comfort, has stretched lighting design to the limit. To fulfill the designer's plan, this space uses all the technology available. Stars, courtesy of fiber optics, change colors as they twinkle. In one area, neon under glass block provides waves of ever-changing color, thanks to an eight-scene dimming system. Undulating bands of neon in rainbow colors constantly move up columns.

Easy maintenance was an absolute requirement, so much of the design uses neon and cold-cathode light sources that will operate for years without maintenance. Bundles of fiber optics, also low maintenance, are glued in the ceiling drywall and connect to metal halide sources with revolving color wheels (that are easy to reach on the third floor for maintenance.)

Halogen accent lighting was installed in the low-ceiling areas, and halogen uplights illuminate the awnings. Cold-cathode light circles the foot of the columns, and the tops of columns hold cold-cathode and purple neon.

This space is truly magical; adults and children alike are drawn to the atrium to watch the slow dance of light across the interior sky.

project
Le Bonheur Children's Medical Center Memphis, TN
lighting
Craig Roeder
architect
J. Wise Smith Associates, Howard K. Smith Associates
interior
Judy Hall
photographer
Robt. Ames Cook

The "ocean floor" turns a humble tunnel into an enchanting passage. An eight-scene dimmer the designer calls a "wave machine" animates neon under the glass brick.

project	**Le Bonheur Children's Medical Center Memphis, TN**
lighting	**Craig Roeder**
architect	**J. Wise Smith Associates, Howard K. Smith Associates**
interior	**Judy Hall**
photographer	**Robt. Ames Cook**

Cold-cathode rings around column feet, guarded by frosted Plexiglas, remain on constantly to satisfy emergency-egress requirements.

project
Le Bonheur Children's Medical Center Memphis, TN
lighting
Craig Roeder
architect
J. Wise Smith Associates, Howard K. Smith Associates
interior
Judy Hall
photographer
Robt. Ames Cook

Like a crayon line, neon sketches the eccentric information desk. The collage of shapes and colors offers a measure of healing relief.

141

project
**Health Central
Orlando, FL**
lighting
Craig Roeder
architect
HKS Inc., Architects
interior
HKS Designcare / Mitchell
photographer
Michael Lowry

[left] Purple neon and 150 PAR38 mercury spots, coupled with dichroic blue color filters, create palm-leaf patterns.

[below left] The lighting design for this nurses station uses a 3200 degrees Kelvin cold cathode to show off the architectural detail of a domed ceiling.

project   **California Pacific Medical Center
            San Francisco, CA**
lighting   **Becca Foster Lighting Design**
architect   **Agnes Bourne Inc.**
interior   **Victoria Stone**
photographer **John Vaughan**

This hospital wanted to create a non-denominational meditation chapel within an existing 15-foot circular space. The small space has furniture and lighting that are flexible enough for private meditation and for occasional gatherings of 10 to 12 people. Existing cove lighting was re-lamped with energy-efficient incandescent lamps. A dimmer increases lamp longevity and lighting adaptability within the multi-purpose space. Some of the existing recessed downlights were re-trimmed and re-lamped to softly wash the faux-marbled surfaces with light.

project	**Milwaukee Heart and Vascular**	The lobby's design centers around a luminous murano glass
	Milwaukee, WI	partition wall that separates the lobby from an inside corridor.
lighting	**Steven L. Klein, Principal;**	Faux-daylight effects mimic the character of natural fenestration,
	Lana M. Nathe	without revealing any of the light sources. An unobstructed,
architect	**The Cerreta Group**	continuous interior, wall-washed by two compact metal-halide
interior	**Marlene King**	floods, provides an even, reflective surface. Wall sconces with
photographer	**Mark F. Heffron**	halogen sources bounce light off of an angled ceiling.

143

project
**UCSF Education Center,
School of Medicine Research
San Francisco, CA**
lighting
David Malman
architect
Bill Diefenbach/ Craig Hamilton
interior
Rebecca Nolan
photographer
Richard Barnes

The renovation of the UCSF Education Center provides new facilities for teaching, research, and interaction, as well as computer and pharmacy labs. A wonderful soft illumination fills this entry and stairway space, while recessed luminaires provide additional light.

project
**Coombs Cancer Center
University of Kentucky
Lexington, KY**
lighting
Lam Partners, Inc.
architect
Omni Architects
interior
The Architects Collaborative
photographer
Dan Danilowicz

The flexibility of this basic lab module is demonstrated by various specialized adaptations. In the daytime, the lab is flooded with daylight, reflected through glazing by light shelves. The clean ceiling provides an ideal surface for indirect illumination, from reflected sunlight and fluorescent light.

project
**Stanford University
MSLS/MRS Research Laboratory
Stanford, CA**
lighting
Architectural Lighting Design
architect
John Rollings / Michael Kelly
interior
Stone, Marraccini & Patterson
photographer
Gregory Murphey

To coax researchers out of labs and into communication with other researchers, the project team designed an exterior personnel corridor on each floor, complete with sunlight, views, and even conversation nooks with chalkboards.

project
Health Central
Orlando, FL
lighting
Craig Roeder
architect
HKS Inc., Architects
interior
HKS Designcare/
Mitchell
photographer
Michael Lowry

The striking architecture comes to life at night as the setting sun casts a fiery glow on the facade.

project   **Greater Baltimore Medical Center**
Acute Care Pavilion
and Women's Medical Center
Baltimore, MD
lighting   **Phase I: Candace M. Kling;**
Phase II: Peter O' Toole
architect   **David R. Beard**
interior   **Teresa Evanko**
photographer   **Maxwell MacKenzie**

[above left] In corridors, trough lighting is used for a softer and less-intimidating effect. The designers avoided the use of bright banks of overhead lights, which would glare harshly into the eyes of patients lying on gurneys.

[above right] This lighting design concept emphasizes hidden and discrete locations for light sources, using both tree branching and floor lamps. Pools of light around the seating and artwork area reinforce the human scale of the spaces.

project
**Cancer Center,
Saint Francis
Hospital and
Medical Center
Hartford, CT**
architect
Carlos Melendez
interior
Allison Miele
photographer
**Warren Jagger
Photography**

[left]   Circulation paths are carefully laid out and articulated with light and color to aid in wayfinding. Indirect cove light provides a good fill light while illuminating the ceiling, helping the space seem open and spacious.

[below]   Here, natural sunlight adds to the lighting plan, making the space relaxing and uplifting.

1. Lobby
2. Office
3. Physician
4. Exam
5. Treatment
6. Planning
7. Dressing
8. Staff lounge

FIRST FLOOR

N ←

project
**Saint Margaret's Center
for Women & Infants
Boston, MA**
lighting
Lam Partners Inc.
architect
Brendan Morrisroe
interior
Renaldo Pesson
photographer
Richard Mandelkorn

The lighting diagram for a typical floor at this hospital grew out of a simple, clear plan for a circulation loop with services grouped in core blocks and patient rooms at the perimeter. The core is wrapped with a neon slot at the ceiling for visual continuity and a low level of ambient lighting. The reception area is punctuated by a series of lighted domes.

medical care facilities

project	**Memorial Hospital of Rhode Island**	The focal point for this project is a new main entrance and lobby.
	Pawtucket, RI	The design objective sought to project an image that would reinforce
lighting	**TRO/The Ritchie Organization**	the hospital's early beginnings. A two-story rotunda, recalling the
architect	**Robert W. Hoye**	architecture of the original main lobby, signals a strong sense of
interior	**Joanne MacIsaac**	permanence and security to those entering the space. The formal
photographer	**Robert Mikrut**	classical style of the space is enhanced by sconces and recessed
		spotlights.

EXTERIOR ENVIRONMENTS

dazzle in the darkness

Good exterior lighting is subtle. It highlights plantings, sculpture, and architecture, without drawing attention to itself. It creates a sense of height and depth, and, most importantly, positive visual impact.

In commercial applications, effective exterior lighting is vital, since profits depend on whether clients, customers, or patrons find their way to places of business. In fact, good lighting

design may be the deciding factor in the success of a business, especially in high-profile endeavors, such as restaurants or nightclubs, where exterior lighting can create the exotic atmosphere that helps an establishment become the popular place to be, instead of just another night spot. And without proper lighting, even the most beautifully designed facade or sign loses its impact at night. Good

exterior lighting can transform a business or public space into a visual landmark that stands out in the crowd.

It's also important to understand that the lighting actually draws people to an entrance. Passersby are drawn to the brightest source of illumination simply by natural tendency. Successful exterior lighting designs exploit this tendency.

In landscaping, lighting design has generally been

overlooked. Huge floodlights and super-bright pole or post lights may provide a lot of illumination, but they do nothing for exterior ambiance. What people end up seeing is a lot of bright glaring lights, and hardly notice the beautiful landscaping or architectural features. Here you will find design techniques and approaches that do their best to capture a piece of the evening sky.

project
**Art Wave '91
Nagoya, Japan**
lighting
**TL Yamagiwa Laboratory,
Nobuyoshi Sakai**
photographer
Yamagiwa Corporation

This sculpture's thousand glowing fiber-optic strands mimic the glow of fireflies.

project **Morning Park Chikara-Machi Nagoya, Japan**

lighting **Kajima Corporation & Kaplan McLaughlin Diaz**

architect **Kajima Corporation & Kaplan McLaughlin Diaz**

photographer **Yamagiwa Corporation**

When evening comes, neighbors come around to this beautiful courtyard for a walk or have a chat with friends. The courtyard is enhanced by the soft glow of the lighting for the waterfall, pond, trees, and corridor to ensure the comfort of the residents of this community through the lighting.

149

Miyazaki Train Station Miyazaki Prefecture Japan

A catalyst for center city development, RTKL's design of Miyazaki Station brings an exuberant, high-tech image to this traditional honeymoon resort on Kyushu Island. Grand in scale but not massive in form, the 9000-square-meter train station comprises three distinct elements: a series of deep-blue towers, a horizontally louvered frame that screens the platform from high winds, and a bright yellow canopy running as a continuous wave along the station's retail promenade. On the interior, undulating forms, tropical colors, and light-colored materials reinforce Miyazaki Station's resort character. The ticket wickets straddle the public concourse to allow continuous circulation between the retail zones at each end of the station.

Using speed and movement as metaphors, RTKL created sail-like exterior lighting fixtures that exploit the theme of travel. During the day, the movement of trains and people flicker through the louvered frame across the facade. At night, dramatic bands of light illuminate this facade, creating a rhythmic palette of light and movement.

Placed along the front edge of a series of blue towers, crescent-shaped vertical lanterns provide a consistent rhythm that contrasts with the movement of the trains. These fixtures have a painted steel frame with both clear and white translucent polycarbonate in fill panels. Fluorescent fixtures are attached to a pulley system allowing them to be lowered for replacement and maintenance, with an access panel in the concrete base of the towers.

The horizontally banded space frame is simply uplit by fixtures extended on bracket arms above the wave canopy. The combination of the perforated aluminum panels and the illuminated space frame produces a "time lapse" appearance. The main entrance, made up of three layers of screens with wavy bands of perforated aluminum panels, is similarly lit. These bands change in appearance depending on the viewing angle. At night, a soft glow emanates from the colored panels of white, yellow, and green.

Through imaginative design and lighting, RTKL has transformed a utilitarian structure into a lively city focal point with popular appeal to commuters, tourists, and residents.

project
Miyazaki Train Station Miyazaki, Japan
lighting
RTKL Associates, Inc.
architect
Michi Yamaguchi
photographer
Steven Hall

Grand in scale but not massive in form, the train station comprises three distinct elements: a series of deep-blue towers, a horizontally louvered frame that screens the platform from high winds, and a bright-yellow canopy running as a continuous wave along the station's retail promenade.

project
Miyazaki Train Station
Miyazaki, Japan
lighting
RTKL Associates, Inc.
architect
Michi Yamaguchi
photographer
Steven Hall

The close-up of the tower shows its delicately lit form. Custom designed tower fixtures give the structure depth and excitement.

MIYAZAKI

19:20

project   **Editel**
             Boston, MA
lighting   **Linda Kondo,**
              Clifford Selbert
photographer **Anton Grassl**

This close-up shows the interrelation of bold lines and vibrant red dots projected with light.

project   **Excalibur**
             Las Vegas, NV
lighting   **John Renton Young**
architect   **Veldon Simpson**
interior   **Marnell Carrao**
photographer **Dave Chawla**

Before its transformation, this "castle" had impressive dimensions, but appeared flat: the wash of illumination produced by the original floodlighting gave the building no depth. The current lighting design includes layers of light that highlight each of the castle's unique architectural features. A combination of focal lighting, floodlighting, and colored lamps creates a make-believe, ethereal mood and enhances the dimensions of the towers.

project
Editel
Boston, MA
lighting
Linda Kondo,
Clifford Selbert
photographer
Anton Grassl

Saturated colors from a light sculpture
turns a building to art.

exterior environments

project
**Westhills Towne Centre
Alberta, Canada**
lighting
**Stebnicki Robertson
and Associates Ltd.**
architect
RTKL Associates Inc.
interior
**Wensley Spotowski
Architectural Group**
photographer
David Whitcomb

Westhills Towne Centre is a single-level neighborhood retail center. The playful building patterns imitate branding-iron and tooled-leather motifs. A monumental pylon evokes regional grain silos. The lighting is designed to let these shapes predominate while calling attention to the setting.

project	**Casino Magic at Biloxi Biloxi, MS**
lighting	**Patrick Gallegos, Principal; Karl Haas**
architect	**Lund & Associates**
interior	**Spectra F/X**
photographer	**Patrick Gallegos**

[below] This simple design approach creates a flexible and dramatic expression by combining existing technology with cutting-edge fixtures. The porte-cochère translucent fabric is underlit with 650-watt halogen lamps covered with dichroic color filters. Two independently controlled colors provide full-color changes, as well as sweeping variations across the translucent canopy. The lighting by reflection also provides the primary light for under the porte-cochère at the casino entry. Additional halogen floods produce focal accents for the escalator entry paths to the casino. Metal halide downlights create functional lighting for an automobile drop-off.

exterior environments

project	**Anzu, Dallas, TX**
lighting	**Paul Draper & Associates**
architect	**Paul Draper & Associates**
interior	**Paul Draper & Associates**
photographer	**Klein & Wilson**

The gray slate wall was designed to draw attention to the entrance and give the visitor a sense of transition from the outer-western world into the restaurant's new and modern Japanese environment. The entry is set back from the street and required establishing presence. The three-foot tall, halo-lit individual letters have a gilded finish and virtually glow with ambient lighting. Up- and down-lighting enhances the rust-colored slate outlining the wall entry's pierced opening. Surrounding lighting helps establish a warm, friendly environment.

project **Stardust**
Las Vegas, NV
lighting **John Renton Young**
architect **Marnell Carrao**
interior **Yates Silverman**
photographer **Dave Chawla**

Magenta neon tubing is laid horizontally across each floor to produce the band of color. The remaining blue-lavender light comes from 1,000-watt lamps around the perimeter of the building's base. Various elements wash the facade. Even illumination is created by using Nema fixtures, custom designed to precision, with adjusted intensity and spread.

project
Stanford University
Parking Structure
Palo Alto, CA
lighting
Watry Design Group
architect
Watry Design Group
photographer
Douglas A. Salin

The dawn sky contrasts strikingly with the H.I.D.-illuminated structure.

project   **PG & E Energy Center**
lighting   **Jim Benya and Deborah Witte,**
              Luminae Souter Lighting Design
architect   **Robinson Mills Williams**
interior   **Robinson Mills Williams**
photographer **Douglas A. Salin**

The Pacific Gas and Electric Energy Center is a learning center open to both design professionals and homeowners. The lower floor houses an almost Disney-like display of alternatives to standard incandescent lighting. The amber glow is a surprise to people who think fluorescent lighting only comes in shades of green. Upstairs, color-corrected fluorescent sources create a shadow-free work environment. The signage is backlit with neon to help lift it from the building facade and give it a "glowing with energy" effect.

project
**East Bay Municipal
Utilities District
Oakland, CA**
lighting
**Jim Benya, Naomi
Miller, Richard Osborn,
Luminae Souter
Lighting Design**
architect
DMJM Hawaii
interior
Whisler Patri
photographer
**Courtesy of Luminae
Souter Lighting Design**

Soft architectural accent lighting in the gazebo, and indirect landscape lighting without, make a relaxed environment for quiet contemplation in this breakout area outside of the meeting rooms.

project
**Wings Kyoto Women's Center
Kyoto, Japan**
lighting
Toshio Tamura
architect
Akira Onishi
interior
Akira Onishi
photographer
Yoshihisa Araki

This building has long been an educational institution for both women's and youth activities. Exterior wall sconces are integrated into architecture; the light sconces are concealed halogen lamps for longer life.

exterior environments

project
**Nations Bank Building
Baltimore, MD**
lighting
Douglas Leigh
architect
RTKL Associates Inc.
photographer
Ron Haisfield

Known as Baltimore's Golden Oldie, the Nations Bank Building was restored to its original beauty in a renovation done in 1994. Copper roof surfaces were cleaned without disturbing their elegant screen patina. New shingles were aged to match their color. Gold leaf was added to recreate the original appearance of the vertical rib members and the crown areas at the top. Dramatic uplighting creates a theatrical appearance at night.

project
**Seafort Square
Tokyo, Japan**
lighting
Shunji Tamai
architect
RIA Co., Ltd.
interior
RIA Co., Ltd.
photographer
**Courtesy of
Shunji Tamai**

Surface- and pole-mounted
fixtures provide exterior
lighting, while uplighting
gives the building a
wonderful presence.
Downlights, from wall
sconces integrated with the
structure, provide security
lighting for pedestrians.

project
**Cranfield Institute
of Technology
Library
Cranfield, England**
lighting
**George Sexton
Associates**
architect
**Sir Norman Foster
and Partners**
interior
**Sir Norman Foster
and Partners**
photographer
Dennis Gilbert

The architectural concept of
"lightness" is accentuated by
a linear fluorescent uplight
system, which highlights the
vaulted ceilings and provides
indirect illumination for the
stacks.

project
Chez Elaine
Copenhagen, Denmark
lighting
Svend Erik Laursen
architect
Courtesy of
Louis Poulsen Lighting
photographer
Kurt Norregaard

The SEL Wall is offered in a
maxi/mini version with a clear or
opal UV-stabilized polycarbonate
globe. It is ideally suited for exterior
lighted areas such as car parks and
business establishments.

project
Pachinko Parlor
Kinbasha, Japan
lighting
Kaoru Mende,
Masahide Kakudate
architect
Kazuyo Sejima
photographer
Nacasa and Partners, Inc.

The yellow-painted wall is provided
with wall washers grouped into a fine
network of circuits that project masses
of light running through the tube with
lightning speed. The glass facade of
the same area as the yellow wall is
emblazoned with logos; "Kinbasha"
is cut from plastic sheets of the
highest diffusibility and transparency.

project
Okazaki Building
Osaka, Japan
lighting
Toshio Tamura
architect
Toshiyuki Sakai and
Koichi Kashiwagi
interior
Toshiyuki Sakai and
Koichi Kashiwagi
photographer
Toshio Kaneko

Custom "tree circle" tree-lighting
fixtures were made for this project.
The fixtures are located inside metal
supports, providing both tree uplight
and ambient light for pedestrians.

project
**Tokyo Design Center
Tokyo, Japan**
lighting
**Kaoru Mende,
Yutaka Inaba**
architect
**Mario Bellini,
Ohbayashi Corp.**
photographer
Toshio Kaneko

This is a showroom building designed by Mario Bellini. Lighting design for this space creates a warm, welcome feeling, reflecting the atmosphere of streets in Italy.

SPECIAL PROJECTS

chapter eleven

The design wonders that fill this chapter did not fit into any of the other categories. Each project stands alone, yet all work together as an all-out celebration of lighting design.

The clients whose projects are collected here, showing complete trust in the design process, have worked in tandem with designers who show wild, unrestrained imagination. As a team, client and designer have integrated lighting seamlessly into overall design strategies, bending the properties of illumination to their creative wills. Light is no longer simply accepted; here, light becomes art. It is being pushed and stretched beyond conventional thinking to break new ground, and it affects viewers in new ways, both conscious and subconscious.

These unorthodox techniques are not typical of commercial spaces. The daring, inventive styles and designs that follow leap the boundaries of the average project to delve into adventure and wonder. These designers break rules, but not without reason. Even spectacular lighting must still be functional, and these projects do an incredible job of combining form with function. Get ready for a trip into the next level of lighting design.

project	**Sportsgirl Centre**
	Melbourne, Australia
lighting	**Hayden McKay**
architect	**Anthony Belluschi**
	Architects, Ltd.
interior	**Communication Arts**
photographer	**Don Dubroff Photography**

Beginning at the retail levels, the atrium rises up through the office levels. It gradually narrows as each floor level extends further into the open space. Each soffit is indirectly lighted with cold cathode housed in coves with perforated metal edges. The atrium is capped with a glazed vertical window that admits natural light throughout the interior of the project.

project
**Sportsgirl Centre
Melbourne, Australia**
lighting
Hayden McKay
architect
**Anthony Belluschi
Architects, Ltd.**
interior
Communication Arts
photographer
**Don Dubroff
Photography**

At Sportsgirl Centre, interior finishes in the retail atrium include marble, tile, bronze, and glass configured to complement the curvilinear atrium. Ceiling lighting, tile patterns, and staircase configurations are coordinated to emphasize the floor-level changes—from the more elegant to the optically energetic lowest level.

project
**St. Louis
Science Center**
St. Louis, MO
lighting
**Robert Osten and
Bill Lam, Lam Partners;
Kiku Obata and
Company**
signage/graphics
**Kiku Obata
and Company**
architect
**E. Verner Johnson
& Associates**
photographer
R. Greg Hursley, Inc.

In daylight, the channel letters
are teal and contrast well with the
white building. At night, they are
backlit and glow bright white.

St. Louis Science Center St. Louis Missouri

When St. Louis selected the
site for its new 150,000-
square-foot science museum,
it presented some unusual
architectural challenges, and
this meant lighting challenges
as well. The plan for the new
building connects it to an
existing planetarium several
hundred feet away, on the
other side of an Interstate.

Architects E. Verner
Johnson and Associates solved
the problem by making a
glass bridge part of the public
exhibit space, complete with
radar guns to clock the speed
of passing traffic. The bridge,
together with a domed Omnimax theater and an overall
"starship" configuration,
produced strong architectural
forms that demanded a strong
lighting response. Lighting
designers Bob Osten and Bill
Lam, of Lam Partners Inc.,
decided that a vocabulary of
neon integrated with the high-
tech architectural elements
would produce the right
exterior lighting expression.
Electric-blue neon mated with
metal tubes traces a meridian
on the dome, and culminates
in an antenna-shaped finial at
the apex. Other neon lines
guide visitors to the
cantilevered canopies of the
main entrance. At the bridge
itself, a neon and acrylic
sandwich forms a continuous
handrail providing soft, reflection free light for the visitors
within the science center, and
a unique signature of the
building for motorists without.

The subtle, contained use
of neon carries through to the
interior as well, with a graphic
and signage system by
Kiku Obata & Company,
incorporating assemblages of
neon, acrylic, aluminum, and
OptiColor glass. The lighting
concepts for the interior keep
the lighting equipment in the
background, and use the light
itself to place visual focus
where it's needed: on the
exhibits and on the special
features of the building.
At the Omnimax theater, for
example, visitors waiting for
the next show gather around a
high, glass-walled projection
room whose huge projector
sparkles with dramatic accent
lighting from unseen sources.
The fascinating equipment is
the focus, not the careful
combination of line and low-
voltage incandescent reflector
lamps tucked out of sight in
slots above the glass wall.

At typical exhibit areas,
the lighting designers and the
architects have worked together
to produce an integrated
system that neatly serves the
needs of mechanical systems,
structure, and flexible lighting.
All this is organized and
partially concealed from view
within the coffers of the precast
concrete "T" structure above.
In place of the conventional
(and expensive) lighting solution
of permanently mounting light
tracks wherever a fixture might
be needed, simple channels
are secured in paired rows
within the ceiling coffers.
Short, portable lengths of light
tracks are then suspended
trapeze-like from these
channels and plugged in only
where they are needed. The
result is great flexibility, in
combination with economy.

The most dramatic lighting
effects are reserved for the
Omnimax theater, where the
lighting systems have the
ability to literally transform the
architectural shape of the
space. Under normal pre-show
conditions, a ring of incandescent PAR lamps uplights the
domed projection surface,
mirroring the soft glow of the
twilight sky. Concealed within
a cove at the dome's base,
these lamps have colored filters
and are controlled in groups
from a central dimming console,
allowing soft fades from white
through sunset hues to a blue
night. But when the show
begins, the space can change
dramatically. The projection
dome is actually made of
perforated metal, and when
the cove lights dim, special-
effects floods and strobes
above the dome can make it
suddenly transparent, revealing
behind it catwalks, supporting
trusses, and all the wizardry of
the 40,000-watt sound system.

project
St. Louis Science Center
St. Louis, MO
lighting
Robert Osten and
Bill Lam, Lam Partners;
Kiku Obata and
Company
architect
E. Verner Johnson
& Associates
photographer
R. Greg Hursley, Inc.

Bundles of fluorescent-green fiber-optics and flashing incandescent lights create the impression that a UFO is blasting off.

project	**Hong Kong Convention Center**
	Hong Kong
lighting	**Motoko Ishii**
architect	**Ng Chun Man and Associates**
interior	**Rocco Design Partners**
photographer	**Motoko Ishii Lighting Design Inc.**

This is the Orient's largest convention and exhibition center, located in the harborside area of Hong Kong. The lighting was designed with an international style, but with a Chinese flavor, and interior detail is used to further enhance the functional lighting, making it even more effective.

special
projects

project
**Bishop International Airport
Flint, MI**
lighting
Robert J. Laughlin
architect
Martin J. Wander
interior
Martin J. Wander
photographer
Neil Rashba

A corridor connecting the airport's landside lobby and "airside" concourse has its own distinct character. The shapes of undulating side windows and ceiling forms are inspired by jet streams. An overhead translucent skylight floods the corridor with light by day, and reflects light from metal halide sources by night. Low-wattage metal halide fixtures with gold reflectors and pewter cones add another layer of illumination. Cove lighting warms the side walls to balance the bright skylit surface. Parabolic fluorescent downlights provide additional illumination and function as emergency lights.

project
Embassy of the Republic of Singapore Wahington, D.C.
lighting
Candace M. Kling
architect
D. Rodman Henderer
interior
Jim Brown
photographer
Allain Jaramillo [right]
Scott McDonald [below]

[right] The lighting in the main lobby/gallery area was designed to accommodate changing art exhibitions. Lighting fixtures are concealed in a recessed trough, allowing them to be re-positioned whenever the artwork is changed.

[below] Light fixtures are disguised by RTKL designed decorative elements, which, in turn, are perceived as lighting the area.

project
Otemachi Financial Center
Tokyo, Japan
lighting
Motoko Ishii
architect
Kume Architects
photographer
Yoichi Yamazaki

The assembly of gold, silver, and bronze pipes are computer-controlled, multicolored lights created by special glass and halogen lamps. The effect is to make the sculpture wave and sparkle, as if breathing.

project
The Mall Himeji
Himeji, Japan
lighting
Motoko Ishii
architect
Yoshimura Architects
photographer
Motoko Ishii Lighting
Design Inc.

The interior of this European-style mall has multi-stories and atria, each with spotlights to provide soft, indirect uplighting, as well as other fixtures to give the floor depth and modulation. In consideration of the surrounding environment, the lowest possible illuminance was used to produce a special ambiance.

project	**University Mall** **Tampa, FL**
lighting	**Gerry Zekowski**
architect	**Anthony Beluschi** **Architects, Ltd.**
interior	**SDI/HTI**
photographer	**George Cott**

The geographic and visual centerpiece of University Mall is its center court, which features an "undersea" tableau of fish, underwater sunlight, and blue-painted and yellow-neon waves. Schools of foam-board fish dangle from the aircraft cable. Curved ceiling forms house light fixtures reminiscent of sparkling sunlight seen from beneath the water's surface. At ground level are wave-shaped fountains with planters and built-in seating.

project
Gifu Memorial Center
World Lightscope
Gifu, Japan
lighting
Motoko Ishii
architect
Nikken Sekkei
Company, Ltd.
photographer
Motoko Ishii
Lighting Design Inc.

[top] The world's largest laser system was installed above the track and field area near the main entrance. Red, green, and blue beams are projected to dance in the night sky over the Memorial Center.

[bottom] Gifu Memorial Center is a sports arena built on the former exposition site. World Lightscope, an integrated performance of light, sound, and images, entertains visitors to the arena. Five giant World Lightscope screens project night scenes from around the world.

定期・積立

project
Tomato Bank
Okayama, Japan
lighting
Iwasaki Electric
architect
Nikken Sekkei
interior
Masanori Umeda
photographer
Nacasa & Partners Inc.

[above]   The round counter communication boards are hung from the ceiling. Information input through computer terminals is displayed here with 24-dot LED lamps. The counter area is lighted from below using fluorescent sources.

[left]   The Tomato Bank logo appears on the ceiling and plays a key role in promotion. Dimmable indirect lighting varies the tone of the space. Lighting on the ceiling is made glareless through the use of diffuse glass. Light sources incorporate fluorescent and H.I.D. lamps, with a few halogen sources.

project
**Osaka Prefectural University
Academic Exchange Hall
Osaka, Japan**
lighting
Yukio Oka
architect
**Osaka Prefecture
Department of Architecture**
interior
**Osaka Prefecture
Department of Architecture**
photographer
Yoshiharu Matsumura

This unique vaulted ceiling is indirectly illuminated by halogen lamps on pole-mounted fixtures and incandescent lamps from recessed fixtures in the wall slit, to provide an even light level for the space.

project
**Nations Bank
Crown Athletic Club
Charlotte, NC**
lighting
Bouyea and Associates, Inc.
architect
HKS Inc.
interior
HKS Interiors
photographer
Ira Montgomery

Architecturally, the stretching area in this club is the anchor between the cardiovascular and fitness areas. The custom light fixture provides more to the project than just functional light; it is the focal point of the space. Colored free-formed glass ribbons give the space energy and life. One lighting circuit provides quartz uplighting for ambient light while the second circuit provides a controlled, intense beam of light through the glass ribbons.

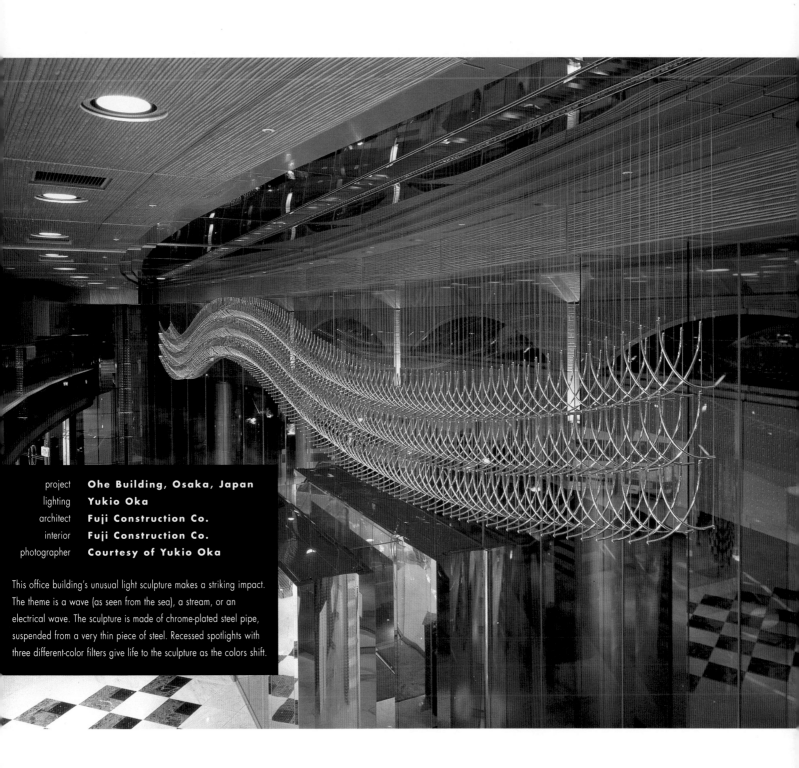

project **Ohe Building, Osaka, Japan**
lighting **Yukio Oka**
architect **Fuji Construction Co.**
interior **Fuji Construction Co.**
photographer **Courtesy of Yukio Oka**

This office building's unusual light sculpture makes a striking impact. The theme is a wave (as seen from the sea), a stream, or an electrical wave. The sculpture is made of chrome-plated steel pipe, suspended from a very thin piece of steel. Recessed spotlights with three different-color filters give life to the sculpture as the colors shift.

special projects

project
**PN Clubhouse
Shibuya, Tokyo**
lighting
TL Yamagiwa Lab.
architect
Osamu Ishiyama
interior
Masanori Umeda
photographer
Yoshio Shiratori

[above] The lounge is illuminated with glare-free, shielded downlights. Compact metal halide sources are used for general illumination, and brightness levels can be changed using an integrated light controller. Halogen lighting can be redirected by remote control.

[right] This multi-purpose space is designed for a business consulting company. It is functionally flexible for events such as meetings, dining, parties, and seminars. Lighting is programmable, and can easily be operated by remote control.

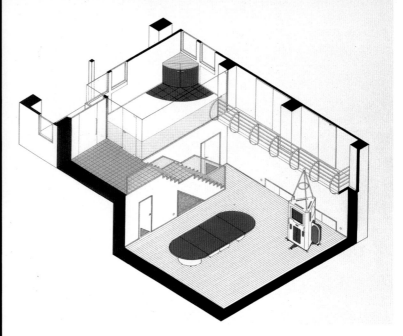

special
projects

project
Irvine City Hall
Irvine, CA
lighting fixture
Poul Henningsen
architect
CRSS, Inc.
interior
Courtesy of
Poulsen Lighting
photographer
John Connell

The PH Louver is a 360-degree glare-free system of perfectly formed graduated reflector shades and concealing cones, supported by four chromated brass struts.

project
The Mall Kasugai
Kasugai, Japan
lighting
Motoko Ishii
architect
M. Yendo
Associated Architects
and Engineers
photographer
Motoko Ishii
Lighting Design Inc.

Exterior lighting uniformly illuminates the interior of the stained-glass atrium mall between the mall buildings, making the mammoth work of art appear to float. Line-lighting on the upper part of the building, and human-scale pole lights, create a lively feeling.

project
Cascade, Private Collection
Long Beach, CA
lighting
Michael Hayden
photographer
Mike Grosswendt

Holographic diffraction grating creates luminous
colors over the surface of the sculpture.

s p e c i a l

p r o j e c t s

project   **Diamond Jim's Premium Place**
             Tropworld Casino and Entertainment Resort
             Atlantic City, NJ
lighting   **Norwood Oliver Design Associates, Inc.**
interior   **Norwood Oliver Design Associates, Inc.**
photographer **Peter Paige**

Contiguous acrylic walls and columns, illuminated from above, encase tiny effervescent bubbles of recirculating water. The kinetic applications and the translucency provide a visual foil, define individual areas and furniture layouts, and provide acoustical and privacy benefits. Shimmering light is reflected throughout the space.

s p e c i a l

p r o j e c t s

project	**East Bay Municipal Utilities District Oakland, CA**	Indirect fluorescent and incandescent lighting in this meeting room provides soft, shadow-free illumination in addition to emphasizing architectural details and finishes.
lighting	**James Benya, Naomi Miller, Richard Osborn, Luminae Souter Lighting Design**	
architect	**DMJM, Hawaii**	
interior	**Whisler Patri**	
photographer	**Courtesy of Luminae Souter Lighting Design**	

project
**Jackpot Casino
Berne, Switzerland**
lighting
**Patrick Galeegos,
Principal;
Nick Pagliante**
architect
Paul Steelman, Ltd.
interior
Paul Steelman, Ltd.
photographer
Nick Pagliante

Here, architectural detail is outlined using low-voltage striplights, which give an elegant sparkle to the space. The dome itself had very restricted space for development of lighting positions, since the painted skyfield is attached in panels directly to the decorative ceiling ribs. Locations at the bottom of the dome and, to a limited degree, at the top of dome, provided space for the dome wash. The wash consists of a custom striplight enclosure, to allow standard low-voltage striplights with color filters to create a horizon glow at the bottom.

project
**Charles E. Smith
Arlington, VA**
lighting
Gensler & Associates
interior
Gensler & Associates
photographer
Tracy Miller

The lighting has been selected to provide a high degree of aesthetics within the constraints of the client s budget. The lighting arrangement is designed to reinforce the fireplace as the main visual focus of the space. Feature lighting includes a pyramidal five- by five-foot faux skylight located above the great hall reception room. Additional lighting includes warm fluorescent cove lighting and uplighting using wall-wash accent units concealed above railwork units that flank the fireplace.

181

Hall E/130-135

project
Moscone Convention Center
San Francisco, CA
lighting
Horton Lees
interior
Gensler & Associates
photographer
Nick Merrick

The ballroom level accesses rooftop
terraces. Fluorescent cove lighting in
concentric tiers provides abundant light
without glare, and gives the impression
of ever-widening space above.

s p e c i a l
p r o j e c t s

project
AT&T Bay Area Special
Services Center
San Francisco, CA
lighting
Randall Whitehead and
Catherine Ng
architect
John Lum, Mike Beam,
Reid & Tarics Associates
interior
John Lum, Mike Beam,
Reid & Tarics Associates
photographer
Christopher Irion

The goal of the clients and the designers was to create a cleanly-designed space with some sparkle and texture, while staying within California's strict Title 24 energy constraints. The 4,100 degrees Kelvin compact fluorescent wall-washers throw light onto the curved metal wall. The shiny band of metal at the top turns the illumination into slashes of light that move with the passers-by as they walk through the space. The buff finish of the corrugated lower portion smooths our the wall-washer's illumination. The open office area toward the rear of the shot is illuminated with pendant-hung indirect metal halide luminaires.

project
**International Institute of
Children's Literature, Osaka
Osaka, Japan**
lighting
Yukio Oka
architect
Shigeru Sugihara
interior
Shigeru Sugihara
photographer
Atelier Fukumoto

Chrome-plated fixtures are located at the tips
of the motif, with halogen lamps to create a
sparkling effect.

s p e c i a l   p r o j e c t s

project
**International Institute of
Children's Literature, Osaka
Osaka, Japan**
lighting
Yukio Oka
architect
Shigeru Sugihara
interior
Shigeru Sugihara
photographer
Atelier Fukumoto

This fan-like light fixture is located in the
second-floor atrium. Its design mimics a group
of people standing in a circle.

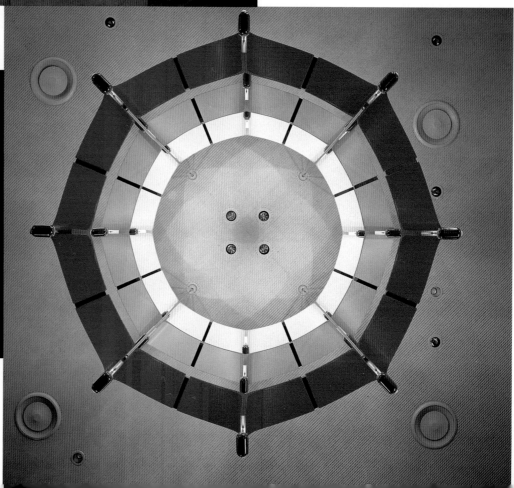

project	**Hiroshima NC Building**
	Hiroshima, Japan
lighting	**Yukio Oka**
architect	**Hajime Okimoto**
interior	**Hajime Okimoto**
photographer	**Bresson Studio**

This entrance has subtle lighting effects that beckon visitors to the door. The uniquely shaped sculptures on stone columns are reflectors made of painted stainless steel. The light source is recessed into the column with sandblasted acrylic diffusers.

directory

architects

Rik Adams
Adams / Mohler Architects
3515 Fremont Avenue N.
Seattle, WA 98103
206-632-2443 Fax: 206-632-9023

Babey—Moulton, Inc.
14 Gold Street
San Francisco, CA 94133
415-394-9910 Fax: 415-394-9920

Backen Arrigoni and Ross Architects
1660 Bush Street
San Francisco, CA 94109
415-441-4771 Fax: 415-536-2333

Mike Beam
Reid and Tarics Associates
55 Hawthorne Street, Suite 400
San Francisco, CA 94105
415-546-7123 Fax: 415-546-7170

David R. Beard, AIA
RTKL Associates Inc.
Commerce Place
One South Street
Baltimore, MD 21202
410-528-8600 Fax: 410-385-2455

Lewis Bedford
Wensley Spotowski Architectural Group
400-237 Eight Avenue, S.E.
Calgary, Alberta T2GOK8
Canada
403-264-7989 Fax: 403-237-5848

David W. Beer
Brennan Beer Gorman / Architects
515 Madison Avenue
New York, NY 10022
212-888-7663 Fax: 212-935-3868

Mario Bellini
Corso Venezia 11 20121
Milano
Italy

Anthony Belluschi, AIA
Anthony Belluschi Architects, Ltd.
55 W. Monroe Street, Suite 200
Chicago, IL 60603
312-236-6751 Fax: 312-782-5191

Andrew Belschner
Andrew Belschner Joseph Vincent
821 Sansome Street
San Francisco, CA 94111
415-982-1215 Fax: 415-982-1220

Agnes C. Bourne, ASID
Agnes C. Bourne, Inc.
Two Henry Adams Street, Space 220
San Francisco, CA 94103
415-626-6883 Fax: 415-626-2489

Cardwell / Thomas & Associates, Inc.
1221 Second Avenue, Suite 300
Seattle, WA 98101
206-622-2311 Fax: 206-442-9165

Jeff Carloss
Jordan Mozer & Associates, Ltd.
228 W. Illinois
Chicago, IL 60610
312-661-0060 Fax: 312-661-0981

Marnell Carrao
4495 Polaris Avenue
Las Vegas, NV 89103
702-736-8577

Paul Carrara
Paul Carrara Restaurant Design
1290 Powell Street
Emeryville, CA 94608
510-547-6763

Sidney C.L. Char
Wimberly Allison Tong & Goo
2222 Kalakana Avenue
Honolulu, HI 96815
808-922-1253 Fax: 808-922-1250

Gene Conti, AIA
Richard Pollack & Associates
214 Grant Avenue, Suite 450
San Francisco, CA 94108
415-788-4400 Fax: 415-788-5309

David Cox, FAIA
KressCox Associates, PC
2909 M Street
Washington, DC 20007
202-965-7070 Fax: 202-965-7144

CRSS Architects, Inc.
444 South Flower Street, 4th Floor
Los Angeles, CA 90071
213-688-3097 Fax: 213-688-2987

John J. Curran, AIA
Torke Wirth & Pujara Ltd.
933 N. Mayfair Road
Wauwatosa, WI 53226
414-453-4554 Fax: 414-453-0682

Ian Curry
Cathedral Architect's Office
The Great Kitchen, The College
Durham, DHI 3EQ
United Kingdom
44-0171-384-7010

Bill Diefenbach, AIA
Stone, Marraccini & Patterson
One Market Plaza
Spear Street Tower, Suite 400
San Francisco, CA 94105
415-227-0100 Fax: 415-495-3223

DMJM Hawaii
1100 Alakea Street, Suite 200
Honolulu, HI 96813
808-538-6747

Tony Doherty
Burg Doherty Bryant & Partners
3rd Floor, Pencardia 1
509 Pretorius Street, Arcadia
Pretoria, 0083 South Africa
27-12-341-6413

Peter Dominick, FAIA
Urban Design Group
1621 18th Street, Suite 200
Denver, CO 80202
303-292-3388 Fax: 303-292-3113

E. Verner Johnson & Associates
222 Berkeley Street, Suite 2100
Boston, MA 02116
617-437-6262 Fax: 617-437-1271

Ehrlich Rominger Architects
4800 El Camino Real
Los Altos, CA 94022
415-949-1300 Fax: 415-941-2209

Einhorn Yaffee Prescott
The Argus Bldg.-Broadway at Beaver
P.O. Box 617
Albany, NY 12201-0617
518-431-3420 Fax: 518-431-3333

ELS / Elbasani & Logan Architects
2040 Addison Court
Berkeley, CA 94704
510-549-2929 Fax: 510-843-3304

Ferraro Choi & Associates, Ltd.
707 Richards Street
Suite 620
Honolulu, HI 96813
808-533-8880 Fax: 808-599-3769

Lloyd Fogelhut, AIA
Sady S. Hashida-Architects
832 Bancroft Way
Berkeley, CA 94710
510-644-2491 Fax: 510-845-3071

C.H. Ned Forrest
Forrest Architects
525 Broadway
Sonoma, CA 95476
707-935-1570

Frank Frost
Frost / Tsuchi Architects
915 Battery Street
San Francisco, CA 94111
415-421-9339

Fuji Construction Co.
1-1-22 Noninbashi, Chuo-ku
Osaka Japan
81-06-946-2241 Fax: 81-06-946-2316

Steve Geiszler
Rupel, Geiszler McLedd
522 Brannan Street
San Francisco, CA 94107
415-243-9440 Fax: 415-243-9490

Gensler & Associates
600 California Street
San Francisco, CA 94108
415-627-3563 Fax: 415-627-3737

Sharad Gokarna
Brennan Beer Gorman Monk / Interiors
515 Madison Avenue
New York, NY 10022
212-888-7663 Fax: 212-935-3868

Peter Gorman, AIA
Brennan Beer Gorman Monk /
Architects
515 Madison Avenue
New York, NY 10022
212-888-7663 Fax: 212-935-3868

Clive Grout, MAIBC
Waisman, Dewar, Grout, Carter
300-1505 West, 2nd Avenue
Vancouver, V6H 3Y4
Canada
604-684-2700

Paul Haigh, AIA
Haigh . Architects . Designers
125 Greenwich Avenue
Greenwich, CT 06830
203-869-5445 Fax: 203-869-5033

Craig Hamilton
Stone, Marraccini & Patterson
225 Arizona Avenue, Suite 3250
Santa Monica, CA 90401
310-458-2080 Fax: 310-458-7393

Naokazu Hanadoh
Shimizu Corporation
Seabanse S., 1-2-3 Shibaura, Minato-ku
Tokyo, 105-07
Japan
81-3-5441-0222 Fax: 81-3-5441-0309

Richard Hannum, AIA
Hannum Associates
222 Sutter Street, Suite 400
San Francisco, CA 94108
415-543-8333 Fax: 415-434-8705

Harper Mackay Ltd.
33-37 Charterhouse Square
London, EC1M 6EA
United Kingdom
0171-600-5151 Fax: 0171-600-1092

D. Rodman Henderer, AIA
RTKL Associates Inc.
Commerce Place
One South Street
Baltimore, MD 21202
410-528-8600 Fax: 410-385-2455

Ray Hirata
Hirata Architects
2719 Tesla Avenue
Los Angeles, CA 90039
213-644-0058

HKS Architects
700 N. Pearl, Suite 1100, LB 307
Dallas, TX 75201
214-969-5599 Fax: 214-969-3284

HOK Inc.
71 Stevenson Street, Suite 2200
San Francisco, CA 94105
415-243-0555 Fax: 415-882-7763

Stephen D. Holzhaver, AIA
Plunkett Raysich Architects
10850 W. Park Place
Suite 300
Milwaukee, WI 53224
414-359-3060 Fax: 414-359-3070

Patty Hopkins, AADip
Michael Hopkins and Partners
27 Broadley Terrace
London, NW1 6LG
England
0171-724-1751 Fax: 0171-723-0932

Michael Hopkins, CBE, RA, AADip, RIBA
Michael Hopkins and Partners
27 Broadley Terrace
London, NW1 6LG England
0171-724-1751 Fax: 0171-723-0932

Horton Lees Lighting Design
1011 Kearny Street
San Francisco, CA 94133
415-986-2575 Fax: 415-986-2576

Robert W. Hoye, AIA
TRO/The Ritchie Organization
80 Bridge Street
Newton, MA 02158
617-969-9400 Fax: 617-527-6753

Huntsman Associates
465 California Street, #1000
San Francisco, CA 94104
415-394-1212 Fax: 415-394-1222

Ikuei Ikeda
Yoshimura Architect & Associates, Inc.
28 Kamimiyanomae-cho, Shishigatani,
Sakyo-ku
Kyoto, 606 Japan
075-771-6071 Fax: 075-761-5937

Interior Architects
350 California Street, Suite 1500
San Francisco, CA 94104
415-434-3305 Fax: 415-434-0330

Osamu Ishiyama
#01 F17 Building no. 51,
3-4-1 Okubo Shinjuku-ku
Tokyo, 169 Japan
03-3203-4141 Fax: 03-3209-8944

J. Wise Smith Associates
771 E. Brookhaven Circle
Memphis, TN 38117
901-767-4135 Fax: 901-767-4298

Robert Jacoubowsky
JHW Architects
299 Cannery Row
Monterey, CA 93940
408-649-1701 Fax: 408-649-3072

Jennifer Johanson, AIA
BarbEric Joint Venture
1414 Fourth Street, Suite 200
San Rafael, CA 94901
415-454-2277 Fax: 415-454-2278

Kajima Corporation
6-5-30 Akasaka, Minato-ku
Tokyo, 107 Japan
81-3-5661-2244 Fax: 81-3-5661-2264

Kaplan McLaughlin Diaz
222 Vallejo Street
San Francisco, CA 94111
415-398-5191 Fax: 415-394-7158

Koichi Kashiwagi
Takenaka Corporation
2-3-10 Nishi Hom-Machi, Nishi-ku
Osaka, 550 Japan
06-252-1201 Fax: 06-538-5415

David Kaspak
Aumiller Youngquist, P.C.
111 E. Busse Avenue, Suite 603
Mt. Prospect, IL 60056
708-253-3761 Fax: 708-394-8320

Michael Kelly
Stone, Marraccini & Patterson
One Market Plaza
Spear Street Tower, Suite 400
San Francisco, CA 94105
415-227-0100 Fax: 415-495-3223

Kennedy Lutz Architecture
764 P Street, Suite B
Fresno, CA 93721
209-497-8035 Fax: 209-497-0872

Pat Kuleto
2350 Marinship Way, #A001
Sausalito, CA 94965
415-331-0880 Fax: 415-331-2954

Kume Architects-Engineers
2-1-22, Shiomi, Koto-ku
Tokyo, 135 Japan
81-3-5632-7811

Kazubiko Kurako
Shimizu Corporation
Seabanse S., 1-2-3 Shibaura, Minato-ku
Tokyo, 105-07 Japan
81-3-5441-0222 Fax: 81-3-5441-0309

Andy Lang
HKS Inc.
700 North Pearl, Suite 1100
Dallas, TX 75201
214-969-5599 Fax: 214-969-3284

Todd B. Lankenau
Lundahl and Associates
1755 E. Plumb Lane, Suite 218
Reno, NV 89502
702-348-7777 Fax: 702-348-0904

Craig Lau, AIA
Miller—Dunwiddie Associates
10340 Viking Drive, Suite 125
Eden Prairie, MN 55344
612-941-0684 Fax: 612-941-0894

Barbara Lazaroff
Imaginings
805 North Sierra Drive
Beverly Hills, CA 90210
310-276-7939 Fax: 310-275-9443

David Leff
David Leff Construction
South Main Street
Sebastopol, CA 95472
707-823-4899

Jim Leggit
RNL Design
1225 17th Street, Suite 1700
Denver, CO 80202
303-295-1717 Fax: 303-292-0845

Robert R. Lowe, AIA, AIJ
Stom Ushidate + Interspace Time
Dai-ni Orient Building
5-13-11 Ueno Taito-ku
Tokyo, 110 Japan
03-3836-7293 Fax: 03-3836-0622

John G.H. Lum
John G.H. Lum Architect
165 Downey Street
San Francisco, CA 94117
415-753-1136 Fax: 415-753-2233

Lund & Associates
1542 E. Beach Boulevard
Gulfport, MS 39501
601-863-8700 Fax: 601-863-4455

Jeffrey A. Lundahl
Lundahl and Associates
1755 E. Plumb Lane, Suite 218
Reno, NV 89502
702-348-7777 Fax: 702-348-0904

M. Yendo Associated Architects and
Engineers
Shiba-Nikkeiyuraku Building, 8th Floor
1-10-13 Shiba, Minato-ku
Tokyo, 105 Japan
81-3-3454-3181 Fax: 81-3-3454-7572

Maki and Associates
3-6-2 Nihonbashi, Chuoh-ku
Tokyo, 103 Japan
03-3274-6681 Fax: 03-3273-4871

Peter Mason
Hill Architects
170 Maiden Lane
San Francisco, CA 94108
415-617-0366 Fax: 415-617-0373

Donald L. Maxcy, ASID
Donald Maxcy Design Associates
The Union Icehouse
600 East Franklin Street
Monterey, CA 93940
408-649-6582 Fax: 408-649-0519

Carlos Melendez, AIA
TRO/The Ritchie Organization
80 Bridge Street
Newton, MA 02158
617-969-9400 Fax: 617-527-6753

Miller Hanson Westerbeck Berger, Inc.
1201 Hawthorne Avenue
Minneapolis, MN 55403
612-332-5420 Fax: 612-332-5425

Joel Miroglio
Miroglio Architecture + Design
381 Orange Street
Oakland, CA 949610
510-891-9145 Fax: 510-891-9107

Mitsubishi Estate Co., Ltd.
2-4-1 Marunouchi, Chiyoda-Ku
Tokyo, Japan
813-3502-4672

Rick Mohler
Adams / Mohler Architects
3515 Fremont Avenue N.
Seattle, WA 98103
206-632-2443 Fax: 206-632-9023

Julia F. Monk, AIA, ASID
Brennan Beer Gorman Monk / Interiors
515 Madison Avenue
New York, NY 10022
212-888-7663 Fax: 212-935-3868

Brendan Morrisroe
TRO/The Ritchie Organization
80 Bridge Street
Newton, MA 02158
617-969-9400 Fax: 617-527-6753

Kazuhiro Motomochi
Tohata Architect & Associates
4-4-10 Fushimi-Cho, Chuo-ku
Osaka Japan
81-06-202-0391 Fax: 81-06-223-1474

Charles Morris Mount
300 W. 108 Street, 2C
New York, NY 10025
212-864-2937 Fax: 212-864-0558

Jordan Mozer
Jordan Mozer & Associates, Ltd.
228 W. Illinois
Chicago, IL 60610
312-661-0060 Fax: 312-661-0981

G.K. Muennig
G.K. Muennig Architect
P.O. Box 92
Big Sur, CA 93920
408-667-2471 Fax: 408-667-2491

Ng Chun Man & Associates
34-35/F Hennessy Centre
Hong Kong
852-2-795-6888

Michael Nicholls
Aumiller Youngquist, P.C.
111 E. Busse Avenue, Suite 603
Mt. Prospect, IL 60056
708-253-3761 Fax: 708-394-8320

Nikken Sekkei Co., Ltd.
4-15-32, Sakae, Naka-ku
Nagoya, 460 Japan
81-52-261-6131

Obayashi Corporation
3-20 Kanda Nishiki Cho, Chiyoda-ku
Tokyo, 101 Japan
81-3-3294-2371 Fax: 81-3-3294-2895

Alan Ohashi
Ohashi Design Studio
5739 Presley Avenue
Oakland, CA 94618
510-652-8840 Fax: 510-652-8604

Joy Ohashi
Ohashi Design Studio
5739 Presley Avenue
Oakland, CA 94618
510-652-8840 Fax: 510-652-8604

Hajime Okimoto
Okimoto Architects Associates
2-5 Tsurumi-cho Naka-ku
Hiroshima Japan
81-082-243-1700 Fax: 81-082-243-1728

Rolf Olhausen, AIA
Prentice & Chan, Ohlhausen Architects
14 E. 4th Street
New York, NY 10012
212-420-8600 Fax: 212-420-9842

Omni Architects
212 N. Upper Street
Lexington, KY 40507
606-252-6664 Fax: 606-253-2358

Akira Onishi
Showa Sekkei, Inc.
1-5-7 Shinmachi Nishi-ku
Osaka, 550 Japan
06-532-3421 Fax: 06-533-1981

Osaka Prefecture
Department of Architecture
Osaka Japan
81-06-941-0351

Michael Ott, AIA
Richard Pollack & Associates
214 Grant Avenue, Suite 450
San Francisco, CA 94108
415-788-4400 Fax: 415-788-5309

OZ Architects
2336 Pearl Street
Boulder, CO 80302
303-449-8900 Fax: 303-449-3886

Jerome Fuentes Paredes
Pacific Custom Finishes
15 B Sumner Street
San Francisco, CA 94103
415-241-0501 Fax: 415-282-7012

Richard Lee Parker, AIA
1581 Masonic Avenue
San Francisco, CA 94117
415-731-7572 Fax: 415-731-1410

Suzanne Parsons
Parsons Design Group
251 Post Street, Suite 412
San Francisco, CA 94104
415-981-0990 Fax: 415-981-3527

Paul Draper & Associates
4106 Swiss Avenue
Dallas, TX 75204
214-824-8352 Fax: 214-824-0932

Paul Steelman, Ltd.
3330 W. Desert Inn Road
Las Vegas, NV 89102
702-873-0221 Fax: 702-367-3565

Bill Pearson
Fee Munson Ebert
500 Montgomery Street
San Francisco, CA 94111
415-434-0320 Fax: 415-434-2409

Cosimo Pizzulli
Pizzulli Associates, Inc.
718 Wilshire Boulevard
Santa Monica, CA 90401-1708
310-393-9572 Fax: 310-458-6156

Christopher Pollock
1000 Steiner Street, Suite 303
San Francisco, CA 94115
415-346-8837

Poulsen Lighting, Inc.
5407 NW 163rd Street
Miami, FL 33014
305-625-1009 Fax: 305-625-1213

Real Restaurants, Inc.
180 Harbor Drive, Suite 100
Sausalito, CA 94965
415-331-9101 Fax: 415-331-9022

RIA (Research Institute of Architecture)
2-12-26 Kohnan Minato-ku
Tokyo, 108 Japan
03-3458-0611 Fax: 03-3458-0610

David Robinson, AIA
Robinson, Mills + Williams
160 Pine Street
San Francisco, CA 94111
415-781-9800 Fax: 415-788-5216

Robinson, Mills + Williams
160 Pine Street
San Francisco, CA 94111
415-781-9800 Fax: 415-788-5216

John Rollings
17 Stetson Avenue
Kentfield, CA 94904
415-258-9044

Gregory Rothweiler
Shea Architects
100 N Sixth Street, Suite 300
Minneapolis, MN 55403
612-339-2257 Fax: 612-349-2930

Ken Rupel
Rupel, Geiszler McLedd
522 Brannan Street
San Francisco, CA 94107
415-243-9440 Fax: 415-243-9490

Toshiyuki Sakkai
Takenaka Corporation
2-3-10 Nishi Hom-Machi, Nishi-ku
Osaka, 550 Japan
06-252-1201 Fax: 06-538-5415

Sato Kogyo
4-12-20 Chuo-ku, Nihonbashi
Tokyo, 103 Japan
03-3661-2949

Rick Schreiber, FARA, IBD
Habitat, Inc.
6031 South Maple Avenue
Tempe, AZ 85283
602-345-8442 Fax: 602-730-0188

Candra Scott
Candra Scott & Associates
30 Langton Street
San Francisco, CA 94103
415-861-0690 Fax: 415-861-0109

Kazuyo Sejima
Kazuyo Sejima Architects & Associates
Yebisu Koyo Heights
2-4-4 Yebisu Minami, Shibuya-ku
Tokyo Japan
81-3-3711-1092 Fax: 81-3-3711-0699

Teresa Sevilla
105 Tunnel Road
Berkeley, CA 94705
510-548-2435 Fax: 510-238-2226

Veldon Simpson
3215 Birtcher Drive
Las Vegas, NV 89118
702-896-1397

Sir Norman Foster and Partners
Riverside Three 22 Hester Road
London, SW11 4AN England
44-171-738-0455 Fax: 44-171-738-1107

Cass Smith
Cass Calder Smith Architecture
522 Second Street
San Francisco, CA 94107
415-546-6470 Fax: 415-546-6415

Peter Smith, MRAIC
Lett Smith Architects
99 Crown Lane
Toronto, Ontario M5R 3P4
Canada
416-968-6990 Fax: 416-924-5780

Robin Snell
Michael Hopkins and Partners
27 Broadley Terrace
London, NW1 6LG England
0171-724-1751 Fax: 0171-723-0932

Barbara Spandorf, AIA
Prentice & Chan, Ohlhausen Architects
14 East 4th Street
New York, NY 10012
212-420-8600 Fax: 212-420-9842

Studios Architecture
99 Green Street
San Francisco, CA 94111
415-398-7575 Fax: 415-398-3829

Shigeru Sugihara
Osaka Prefecture, Dept. of Architecture
Osaka Japan
81-06-941-0351

Taisei Corporation
Shinjyuku Center Building
1-25-1, Nishi-shinjyuku, Shinjyuku-ku
Tokyo, 163 Japan
81-3-3348-1111

Takenaka Corporation
1-21-8 Ginza, Chuo-ku
Tokyo, 104 Japan
81-3-3542-7100

Seiji Tanaka
Yoshimura Architect & Associates, Inc.
28 Kamimiyanomae-cho,
Shishigatani, Sakyo-ku
Kyoto, 606 Japan
075-771-6071 Fax: 075-761-5937

The Seiyo Corporation
Sunshine 60 33F
3-1-1 Higashi Ikebukuro, Toshima-ku
Tokyo, 170 Japan
81-3-3984-2214 Fax: 81-3-3984-9274

Larry Traxler
Jordan Mozer & Associates, Ltd.
228 W. Illinois
Chicago, IL 60610
312-661-0060 Fax: 312-661-0981

Joseph Vincent
Andrew Belschner Joseph Vincent
821 Sansome Street
San Francisco, CA 94111
415-982-1215 Fax: 415-982-1220

Martin J. Wander, AIA
Reynolds, Smith and Hills, Inc.
4651 Salisbury Road
Jacksonville, FL 32256
904-279-2425 Fax: 904-279-2491

Ward Young Architects
12010 Donner Pass Road
Truckee, CA 96161
916-587-3859 Fax: 916-587-8908

Watry Design Group
1500 Fashion Island Boulevard #200
San Mateo, CA 94404
415-349-1546 Fax: 415-349-1384

John Webster
Wensley Spotowski Architectural Group
5555 Calgary Trail, Suite 1050
Calgary, Alberta TGH5P9
Canada
403-438-2404 Fax: 403-435-0151

Whisler-Patri
Two Bryant Street
San Francisco, CA 94105
415-957-0200 Fax: 415-777-4394

Whitfield Partners
63/67 Carter Lane
London, EC4 5HE
United Kingdom

William Tabler and Associates
333 7th Avenue
New York, NY 100031-5004
212-563-6960 Fax: 212-563-3322

Wimberly Allison Tong & Goo
2260 University Drive
Newport Beach, CA 92660
714-574-8500 Fax: 714-574-8550

Tom Witte, AIA
The Cerreta Group
235 W. Broadway - Rotunda Landmark
Waukesha, WI 53186
414-544-2044 Fax: 414-544-4201

Wil Wong
Wil Wong Associates
2710 Webster Street
San Francisco, CA 94123
415-346-7700

Evans Woollen
Woollen, Molzan and Partners, Inc.
47 South Pennsylvania Street,
10th Floor
Indianapolis, IN 46204
317-632-7484 Fax: 317-687-2064

Jack J. Worstell, AIA
Hornberger + Worstell
170 Maiden Lane, Suite 170
San Francisco, CA 94108
415-391-1080 Fax: 415-986-6387

Kei Yamagami
Gensler & Associates
600 California Street
San Francisco, CA 94108
415-627-3563 Fax: 415-627-3737

Michi Yamaguchi, AIA
RTKL Associates Inc.
Commerce Place, One South St.
Baltimore, MD 21202
410-528-8600 Fax: 410-385-2455

Yamashita Sekkei Inc.
Ohmori Belport Building A
1-26-6 Minami-ohi, Shinagawa-ku
Tokyo, 140 Japan
81-3-5471-5561

Ryuichi Yokogawa
Nikken Sekkei, Ltd.
6-2, 4-Chome, Koraibashi, Chuo-ku
Osaka, 541 Japan
06-203-2361 Fax: 06-203-4277

Yoshimura Architects
28 Shishigatani Kami, Miyanomae-cho,
Sakyo-hu, Kyoto, 606 Japan
81-75-771-6071

Moore Rubell Yudell
933 Pico Boulevard
Santa Monica, CA 90405
310-450-1400 Fax: 310-450-1403

Nicholas P. Zalany
Richard P. Jencen Associates
2850 Euclid Avenue
Cleveland, OH 44115
216-781-0131 Fax: 216-781-0134

interior

Adams / Mohler Architects
3515 Fremont Avenue N.
Seattle, WA 98103
206-632-2443 Fax: 206-632-9023

Ron Aguila
Simon Martin-Vegue Winkelstein Moris
501 Second Street
San Francisco, CA 94107
415-546-0400 Fax: 415-882-7098

Barbara Allen
SL + A Hotels Group
1001 Tai Sang Bldg.
24-34 Henessy Road
Hong Kong
852-2528-5544 Fax: 852-2861-0354

Architectural Interiors
162 Parliament Street
Toronto, Ontario M5E 221 Canada
416-367-9144 Fax: 416-367-9151

Nancy Arriano, ASID
Plunkett Raysich Architects
10850 W. Park Place, Suite 300
Milwaukee, WI 53224
414-359-3060 Fax: 414-359-3070

Babey—Moulton, Inc.
14 Gold Street
San Francisco, CA 94133
415-394-9910 Fax: 415-394-9920

Backen Arrigoni and Ross Architects
1660 Bush Street
San Francisco, CA 94109
415-441-4771 Fax: 415-536-2333

Mike Beam
Reid and Tarics Associates
55 Hawthorne Street, Suite 400
San Francisco, CA 94105
415-546-7123 Fax: 415-546-7170

Jo Anna Becker
Brennan Beer Gorman Monk/Architects
515 Madison Avenue
New York, NY 10022
212-888-7663 Fax: 212-935-3868

David W. Beer, AIA
Brennan Beer Gorman/Architects
515 Madison Avenue
New York, NY 10022
212-888-7663 Fax: 212-935-3868

David Birn
Skylight Opera Theatre Artists
158 North Broadway
Milwaukee, WI 53202
414-291-7811

Jim Brown, AIA
RTKL Associates Inc.
Commerce Place
One South Street
Baltimore, MD 21202
410-528-8600 Fax: 410-385-2455

Marnell Carrao
4495 Polaris Avenue
Las Vegas, NV 89103
702-736-8577

Paul Carrara
Paul Carrara Restaurant Design
1290 Powell Street
Emeryville, CA 94608
510-547-6763

Communication Arts
1112 Pearl Street
Boulder, CO 80302-5196
303-447-8202 Fax: 303-440-7096

CRSS Architects, Inc.
444 South Flower Street, 4th Floor
Los Angeles, CA 90071
213-688-3097 Fax: 213-688-2987

Richard D'Amico
D'Amico and Partners Inc.
1402 First Avenue S.
Minneapolis, MN 55403
612-334-3366

Daiko Corporation
3-15-16 Nakamichi Higashinari-ku
Osaka, 537 Japan
06-972-5555 Fax: 06-974-5569

Lorrie Dalton
Media Five Limited
345 Queen Street
Honolulu, HI 96813
808-524-2040 Fax: 808-538-1529

George DeWitt
Parsons Design Group
251 Post Street, Suite 412
San Francisco, CA 94104
415-981-0990 Fax: 415-981-3527

Mike Doyle
Communication Arts Inc.
1112 Pearl Street
Boulder, CO 80302
303-447-8202 Fax: 303-440-7096

David Ebert
Fee Munson Ebert
500 Montgomery Street
San Francisco, CA 94111
415-434-0320 Fax: 415-434-2409

Einhorn Yaffee Prescott
The Argus Bldg.-Broadway at Beaver
P.O. Box 617
Albany, NY 12201-0617
518-431-3420 Fax: 518-431-3333

Eric Engstrom, IIDA
BarbEric Joint Venture
1414 Fourth Street, Suite 200
San Rafael, CA 94901
415-454-2277 Fax: 415-454-2278

Fumio Enomoto
Enomoto Atelier
2-28-31 Chuo, Nakano-ku
Tokyo, 164 Japan
81-3-5330-5696 Fax: 81-3-5330-5727

Teresa Evanko, AIA
RTKL Associates Inc.
Commerce Place, One South Street
Baltimore, MD 21202
410-528-8600 Fax: 410-385-2455

Forrest Architects
525 Broadway
Sonoma, CA 95476
707-935-1570

Richard Foy
Communication Arts Inc.
1112 Pearl Street
Boulder, CO 80302
303-447-8202 Fax: 303-440-7096

Janet Gay Freed
Janet Freed Interior Design
295 South Street
Sausalito, CA 94965
415-332-2572 Fax: 415-332-7015

Frost / Tsuchi Architects
915 Battery Street
San Francisco, CA 94111
415-421-9339

Fuji Construction Co.
1-1-22 Noninbashi, Chuo-ku
Osaka, Japan
81-06-946-2241 Fax: 81-06-946-2316

Kenny Fukumoto
P.O. Box 2639
Carmel, CA 93921
408-624-0765

Mikio Furusawa
Nikken Sekkei Ltd.
6-2, 4-Chome, Koraibashi, Chuo-ku
Osaka, Japan
06-203-2655 Fax: 06-203-5967

Gandy / Peace, Inc.
3195 Paces Ferry Place, N.W.
Atlanta, GA 30305-1307
404-237-8681 Fax: 404-237-6150

Steve Geiszler
Rupel, Geiszler McLedd
522 Brannan Street
San Francisco, CA 94107
415-243-9440 Fax: 415-243-9490

Gensler & Associates
600 California Street
San Francisco, CA 94108
415-627-3563 Fax: 415-627-3737

Charles Grebmeier, ASID
Grebmeier and Associates
1298 Sacramento Street
San Francisco, CA 94108
415-931-1088 Fax: 415-373-5409

Barbara Haigh
Haigh . Architects . Designers
125 Greenwich Avenue
Greenwich, CT 06830
203-869-5445 Fax: 203-869-5033

Paul Haigh, AIA
Haigh . Architects . Designers
125 Greenwich Avenue
Greenwich, CT 06830
203-869-5445 Fax: 203-869-5033

Jessica Hall
Jessica Hall Associates
1301 6th Street, Suite G
San Francisco, CA 94107
415-552-9923 Fax: 415-552-9963

Judy Hall c/o Le Bonheur Hospital
50 N. Dunlap Street
Memphis, TN 38103
901-572-3000

Richard Hannum, AIA
Hannum Associates
222 Sutter Street, Suite 400
San Francisco, CA 94108
415-543-8333 Fax: 415-434-8705

Harper Mackay Ltd.
33-37 Charterhouse Square
London, EC1M 6EA United Kingdom
0171-600-5151 Fax: 0171-600-1092

Sady S. Hashida, AIA, AAA&E, NCARB, CSI
Sady S. Hashida-Architects
832 Bancroft Way
Berkeley, CA 94710
510-644-2491 Fax: 510-845-3071

Hirsh Bedner Associates
3216 Nebraska Avenue
Santa Monica, CA 90404
310-829-9087 Fax: 310-453-1182

HKS Designcare/Medical Space Design
700 N. Pearl, Suite 1100, LB 307
Dallas, TX 75201
214-969-5599

Interior Architects
350 California Street, Suite 1500
San Francisco, CA 94104
415-434-3305 Fax: 415-434-0330

Robert Josten
2640 Huron Street
Los Angeles, CA 90065
213-221-1237

Koichi Kashiwagi
Takenaka Corporation
2-3-10 Nishi Hom-Machi, Nishi-ku
Osaka, 550 Japan
06-252-1201 Fax: 06-538-5415

Hiroshi Kawaguchi
Yoshimura Architect & Associates, Inc.
28 Kamimiyanomae-cho, Shishigatani,
Sakyo-ku
Kyoto, 606 Japan
075-771-6071 Fax: 075-761-5937

Marlene King
864 Honey Creek Parkway
Wauwatosa, WI 53214
414-4475-6879

Yasuo Kondo
Yasuo Kondo Design Office
Bond St. T-3 2F,
2-2-43 Higashi Shinagawa,
Shinagawa-ku
Tokyo, 140 Japan
81-3-3458-1185 Fax: 81-3-3458-1187

Pat Kuleto
2350 Marinship Way, #A001
Sausalito, CA 94965
415-331-0880 Fax: 415-331-2954

Barbara Lazaroff
Imaginings
805 North Sierra Drive
Beverly Hills, CA 90210
310-276-7939 Fax: 310-275-9443

John Lum
Reid and Tarics Associates
55 Hawthorne Street, Suite 400
San Francisco, CA 94105
415-546-7123 Fax: 415-546-7170

John G.H. Lum
John Lum Architecture
165 Downey Street,
San Francisco, CA 94117
415-753-1136 Fax: 415-753-2233

Joanne MacIsaac, ASID, IBD
TRO/The Ritchie Organization
80 Bridge Street
Newton, MA 02158
617-969-9400 Fax: 617-527-6753

James Marzo
James Marzo Design
251 Rhode Island Street, Suite 211
San Francisco, CA 94103
415-626-7250 Fax: 415-626-7260

Donald L. Maxcy, ASID
Donald Maxcy Design Associates
The Union Icehouse
600 East Franklin Street,
Monterey, CA 93940
408-649-6582 Fax: 408-649-0519

Ann McKenzie
Habitat, Inc.
6031 South Maple Avenue
Tempe, AZ 85283
602-345-8442 Fax: 602-730-0188

Joszi Meskan
Joszi Meskan Associates
479 Ninth Street
San Francisco, CA 94010
415-431-0500 Fax: 415-431-9339

Allison Miele, IBD
TRO/The Ritchie Organization
80 Bridge Street
Newton, MA 02158
617-969-9400 Fax: 617-527-6753

Joel Miroglio
Miroglio Architecture + Design
381 Orange Street
Oakland, CA 949610
510-891-9145 Fax: 510-891-9107

Michael Moore
Michael Moore Design
2100 Jackson Street
San Francisco, CA 94115
415-567-7955 Fax: 415-567-7956

Lamberto Moris
Simon Martin-Vegue Winkelstein Moris
501 Second Street
San Francisco, CA 94107
415-546-0400 Fax: 415-882-7098

Saburo Morishima
Nikken Sekkei Ltd.
6-2, 4-Chome, Koraibashi, Chuo-ku
Osaka Japan
06-203-2655 Fax: 06-203-5967

Kazuhiro Motomochi
Tohata Architect & Associates
4-4-10 Fushimi-cho, Chuo-ku
Osaka Japan
81-06-202-0391 Fax: 81-06-223-1474

Charles Morris Mount
300 W. 108 Street, 2C
New York, NY 10025
212-864-2937 Fax: 212-864-0558

Jordan Mozer
Jordan Mozer & Associates, Ltd.
228 W. Illinois
Chicago, IL 60610
312-661-0060 Fax: 312-661-0981

Seiichi Nakagawa
MHS Planners, Architects & Engineers
1-5-17 Motoasaka Minato-ku
Tokyo, 107 Japan
03-3403-6161 Fax: 03-3403-6780

Wendy Neumeister
Aumiller Youngquist, P.C.
111 E. Busse Avenue, Suite 603
Mt. Prospect, IL 60056
708-253-3761 Fax: 708-394-8320

Michael Nicholls
Aumiller Youngquist, P.C.
111 E. Busse Avenue, Suite 603
Mt. Prospect, IL 60056
708-253-3761 Fax: 708-394-8320

Brian O Flynn
Murphy O Flynn Design Associates
736 Clementina Street, Suite 330
San Francisco, CA 94103
415-626-7845 Fax: 415-626-7848

Alan Ohashi
Ohashi Design Studio
5739 Presley Avenue
Oakland, CA 94618
510-652-8840 Fax: 510-652-8604

Joy Ohashi
Ohashi Design Studio
5739 Presley Avenue
Oakland, CA 94618
510-652-8840 Fax: 510-652-8604

Keizo Okazaki
Takamashiya- Dept. of Interior
Architecture
3-5-25 Nihonbashi, Naniwa-ku
Osaka Japan
81-06-632-3091 Fax: 81-06-632-9147

Hajime Okimoto
Okimoto Architects Associates
2-5 Tsurumi-cho Naka-ku
Hiroshima Japan
81-082-243-1700 Fax: 81-082-2443-1728

Rolf Olhausen, AIA
Prentice & Chan, Ohlhausen Architects
14 E. 4th Street
New York, NY 10012
212-420-8600 Fax: 212-420-9842

Norwood Oliver
Norwood Oliver Design Associates, Inc.
65 Bleecker Street
New York, NY 10012
212-982-7050 Fax: 212-674-2302

Akira Onishi
Showa Sekkei, Inc.
1-5-7 Shinmachi Nishi-ku
Osaka, 550 Japan
06-532-3421 Fax: 06-533-1981

Osaka Prefecture
Department of Architecture
Osaka Japan
81-06-941-0351

Jerome Fuentes Paredes
Pacific Custom Finishes
15 B Sumner Street
San Francisco, CA 94103
415-241-0501 Fax: 415-282-7012

Richard Lee Parker, AIA
1581 Masonic Avenue
San Francisco, CA 94117
415-731-7572 Fax: 415-731-1410

Suzanne Parsons
Parsons Design Group
251 Post Street, Suite 412
San Francisco, CA 94104
415-981-0990 Fax: 415-981-3527

Paul Draper & Associates
4106 Swiss Avenue
Dallas, TX 75204
214-824-8352 Fax: 214-824-0932

Paul Steelman, Ltd.
3330 W. Desert Inn Road
Las Vegas, NV 89102
702-873-0221 Fax: 702-367-3565

Renaldo Pesson
TRO/The Ritchie Organization
80 Bridge Street
Newton, MA 02158
617-969-9400 Fax: 617-527-6753

Cosimo Pizzulli
Pizzulli Associates, Inc.
718 Wilshire Boulevard
Santa Monica, CA 90401-1708
310-393-9572 Fax: 310-458-6156

Carol Podham
Simon Martin-Vegue Winkelstein Moris
501 Second Street
San Francisco, CA 94107
415-546-0400 Fax: 415-882-7098

Eugene Potente, Jr., ASID
The Studios of Potente
914 60th Street
Kenosha, WI 53140
414-654-3535

Poulsen Lighting, Inc.
5407 N.W. 163rd Street
Miami, FL 33014
305-625-1009 Fax: 305-625-1213

Real Restaurants, Inc.
180 Harbor Drive, Suite 100
Sausalito, CA 94965
415-331-9101 Fax: 415-331-9022

RIA (Research Institute of Architecture)
2-12-26 Kohnan Minato-ku
Tokyo, 108 Japan
03-3458-0611 Fax: 03-3458-0610

Chuck Roberts
BRC Imagination Arts
824 North Victory Boulevard
Burbank, CA 91502
818-841-8084

Robinson, Mills + Williams
160 Pine Street
San Francisco, CA 94111
415-781-9800 Fax: 415-788-5216

Rocco Design Partners
Room 4201 Hopewell Centre,
17 Kennedy Road
Hong Kong, 5-280128
81-3-3353-5120

Bob Rogers
BRC Imagination Arts
824 North Victory Boulevard
Burbank, CA 91502
818-841-8084

Ken Rupel
Rupel, Geiszler McLedd
522 Brannan Street
San Francisco, CA 94107
415-243-9440 Fax: 415-243-9490

Toshiyuki Sakkai
Takenaka Corporation
2-3-10 Nishi Hom-Machi, Nishi-ku
Osaka, 550 Japan
06-252-1201 Fax: 06-538-5415

Bruno Schloffel
Gart Sports
1000 Broadway
Denver, CO 80203
303-861-1122

John Schneider, ASID
John Schneider Environmental Design
P.O. Box 1457
Pebble Beach, CA 93953
408-649-8221 Fax: 408-655-1093

Candra Scott
Candra Scott & Associates
30 Langton
San Francisco, CA 94103
415-861-0690 Fax: 415-861-0109

SDI/HTI
311 Elm Street, Suite 600
Cincinnati, OH 45202-2706
513-241-3000 Fax: 513-241-5015

Laura Seccombe
Seccombe Design Associates
126 South Park
San Francisco, CA 94107
415-957-9882 Fax: 415-543-1349

Yoshio Shibata
Nikken Sekkei Ltd.
6-2, 4-Chome, Koraibashi, Chuo-ku
Osaka Japan
06-203-2655 Fax: 06-203-5967

Yates Silverman
4045 Industrial Road
Las Vegas, NV
702-791-5606

Sir Norman Foster and Partners
Riverside Three 22 Hester Road
London, SW11 4AN England
44-171-738-0455 Fax: 44-171-738-1107

Cass Smith
Cass Calder Smith Architecture
522 Second Street
San Francisco, CA 94107
415-546-6470 Fax: 415-546-6415

William Spack
KressCox Associates, PC
2909 M Street
Washington, DC 20007
202-965-7070 Fax: 202-965-7144

Barbara Spandorf, AIA
Prentice & Chan, Ohlhausen Architects
14 E. 4th Street
New York, NY 10012
212-420-8600 Fax: 212-420-9842

Spectra F/X
1270 Avenida Acaso
Camarillo, CA 93012
805-388-5246 Fax: 805-484-8529

Sylvia Stevens
Sylvia Stevens and Associates
2356 Jones Street
San Francisco, CA 94133
415-474-5815 Fax: 415-474-5225

Victoria Stone
Victoria Stone Interiors
893 Noe Street
San Francisco, CA 94114
415-826-0904

Stone, Marraccini & Patterson
One Market Plaza
Spear Street Tower, Suite 400
San Francisco, CA 94105
415-227-0100 Fax: 415-495-3223

Studios Architecture
99 Green Street
San Francisco, CA 94111
415-398-7575 Fax: 415-398-3829

Shigeru Sugihara
Osaka Prefecture, Dept. of Architecture
Osaka Japan
81-06-941-0351

Christ Surunis
Davis Design Group
318 Harrison Street, Suite 202
Oakland, CA 94607
510-832-0702 Fax: 510-832-0704

Gene Takeshita
P.O. Box 22407
Monterey, CA 93922
408-655-1244 Fax: 408-655-0533

Seiji Tanaka
Yoshimura Architect & Associates, Inc.
28 Kamimiyanomae-cho, Shishigatani,
Sakyo-ku
Kyoto, 606 Japan
075-771-6071 Fax: 075-761-5937

The Architects Collaborative
46 Brattle Street
Cambridge, MA 02138
617-868-4200 Fax: 617-868-4226

The Malder Company
1157 Folsom Street
San Francisco, CA 94103
415-626-9492 Fax: 415-626-9693

Laura Tredinnick, IES
Schuler & Shook, Inc.
123 Third Street N., Suite 216
Minneapolis, MN 55401
612-339-5958 Fax: 612-941-0894

Masanori Umeda
U-Meta Design, Inc.
1-8-3 Nishiazabu, Minato-ku
Tokyo, 108 Japan
03-3401-0328 Fax: 03-3401-0783

Stom Ushidate, DDA, JCD
Stom Ushidate + Interspace Time
Dai-ni Orient Building
5-13-11 Ueno Taito-ku
Tokyo, 110 Japan
03-3836-7293 Fax: 03-3836-0622

Sue Wade
HKS Interiors
700 North Pearl, Suite 1100
Dallas, TX 75201
214-969-5599 Fax: 214-969-3284

Martin J. Wander, AIA
Reynolds, Smith and Hills, Inc.
4651 Salisbury Road
Jacksonville, FL 32256
904-279-2425 Fax: 904-279-2491

Whisler—Patri
Two Bryant Street
San Francisco, CA 94105
415-957-0200 Fax: 415-777-4394

William Whistler, AIA
Brennan Beer Gorman Monk / Interiors
515 Madison Avenue
New York, NY 10022
212-888-7663 Fax: 212-935-3868

Whitfield Partners
63/67 Carter Lane
London, EC4 5HE
United Kingdom

Trisha Wilson
Trisha Wilson & Associates
3811 Turtle Creek Boulevard, 15th Floor
Dallas, TX 75219
214-521-6753 Fax: 214-521-0207

Barbara Wofling
BarbEric Joint Venture
1414 Fourth Street, Suite 200
San Rafael, CA 94901
415-454-2277 Fax: 415-454-2278

Woollen, Molzan and Partners, Inc.
47 South Pennsylvania Street, 10th Floor
Indianapolis, IN 46204
317-632-7484 Fax: 317-687-2064

George Yabu
Yabu Pushelberg
55 Booth Avenue
Toronto, Ontario M4M 2M3
Canada
416-778-9779 Fax: 416-778-9747

Lydia Young
Communication Arts Inc.
1112 Pearl Street
Boulder, CO 80302
303-447-8202 Fax: 303-440-7096

Nicholas P. Zalany
Richard P. Jencen Associates
2850 Euclid Avenue
Cleveland, OH 44115
216-781-0131 Fax: 216-781-0134

David Zinn
Skylight Opera Theatre Artists
158 North Broadway
Milwaukee, WI 53202
414-291-7811

lighting

Pam Ackerman
Design Lighting Resource, Inc.
8361 East Evans, Suite 108
Scotsdale, AZ 85260
602-991-5655 Fax: 602-991-6064

Adams / Mohler Architects
3515 Fremont Avenue N.
Seattle, WA 98103
206-632-2443 Fax: 206-632-9023

Architectural Lighting Design
370 Brannan Street
San Francisco, CA 94107
415-495-4085 Fax: 415-4495-4660

Len Auerbach, ASTC
S. Leonard Auerbach & Associates, Inc.
1045 Sansome St.reet, #218
San Francisco, CA 94111
415-392-7528 Fax: 415-392-7530

Aumiller Youngquist, P.C.
111 E. Busse Avenue, Suite 603
Mt. Prospect, IL 60056
708-253-3761 Fax: 708-394-8320

Backen Arrigoni and Ross Architects
1660 Bush Street
San Francisco, CA 94109
415-441-4771 Fax: 415-441-8360

Hiram Banks, LIT
Lighting Integration Technology, Inc.
10 Arkansas Street
San Francisco, CA 94107
415-863-0313 Fax: 415-863-3923

Vladimir Bazjanac, Ph.D.
UC Berkeley
P.O. Box 4158
Berkeley, CA 94704
510-548-4440

Leonor Bedel, IALD
Leonor Bedel & Associates
Avda. Juan De Garay 325 4β7
Buenos Aires, 1153 Argentina
541-361-9792 Fax: 541-361-3451

Jim Benya
Benya Lighting Design
3491 Cascade Terrace
West Linn, OR 97068
503-657-9157 Fax: 503-657-9153

Bradley A. Bouch, IESNA
JRY Lighting & Sign
3665 W. Diablo
Las Vegas, NV 89118
702-739-6789 Fax: 702-739-9618

Barbara Bouyea, IES
Bouyea & Associates, Inc.
3811 Turtle Creek Boulevard, Suite 1010
Dallas, TX 75219
214-520-6580 Fax: 214-520-6531

Teal Brogden
Horton Lees Lighting Design
1011 Kearny Street
San Francisco, CA 94133
415-986-2575 Fax: 415-986-2576

Edward J. Cansino
Edward J. Cansino & Associates
1620 School Street, Suite 102
Moraga, CA 94556
510-376-9497 Fax: 510-376-9498

Stephanie B. Cissna
7641 S.E. Harrison
Portland, OR 97215
503-777-3817

Clanton Engineering
4699 Nautilus Court South, Suite 101
Boulder, CO 80301
303-530-7229 Fax: 303-530-7227

Ross De Alessi
Ross De Alessi Lighting Design
2815 Second Avenue, Suite 280
Seattle, WA 98121
206-441-0870 Fax: 206-441-9926

Michael DiBlasi, USITT
Schuler & Shook, Inc.
123 Third Street N., Suite 216
Minneapolis, MN 55401
612-339-5958 Fax: 612-337-5097

David Ebert
Horton Lees Lighting Design
1011 Kearny Street
San Francisco, CA 94133
415-986-2575 Fax: 415-986-2576

Wallace G. Eley, IES, PEO
Crossey Engineering Ltd.
4141 Yonge Street, Suite 305
Toronto, Ontario M2P 2A8
Canada
416-221-3111 Fax: 416-221-4354

Linda Ferry, IES, ASID
Architectural Illumination
P.O. Box 2690
Monterey, CA 93942
408-649-3711 Fax: 408-375-5897

Lloyd Fogelhut, AIA
Sady S. Hashida-Architects
832 Bancroft Way
Berkeley, CA 94710
510-644-2491 Fax: 510-845-3071

Becca Foster, DLF, IES
Becca Foster Lighting
27 South Park
San Francisco, CA 94107
415-541-0370 Fax: 415-957-5856

Larry French, IALD, IES, USITT
S. Leonard Auerbach & Associates, Inc.
1045 Sansome Street
San Francisco, CA 94111
415-392-7528 Fax: 415-392-7530

Patrick Gallegos
Gallegos Lighting Design
8132 Andasol Avenue
Northridge, CA 91325
818-343-5762 Fax: 818-343-2041

Gandy / Peace, Inc.
3195 Paces Ferry Place N.W.
Atlanta, GA 30305-1307
404-237-8681 Fax: 404-237-6150

Gensler & Associates
600 California Street
San Francisco, CA 94108
415-627-3563 Fax: 415-627-3737

Patricia Glasow, IALD
S. Leonard Auerbach & Associates, Inc.
1045 Sansome Street, #218
San Francisco, CA 94111
415-392-7528 Fax: 415-392-7530

Stefan Graf, IALD, IES
Illuminart
404 North River
Ypsilanti, MI 48198
313-482-6066 Fax: 313-482-0324

Marty Gregg
Weber Design, Inc.
1439 Larimer Square
Denver, CO 80202
303-892-9816 Fax: 303-892-7753

Karl Haas
Gallegos Lighting Design
8132 Andasol Avenue
Northridge, CA 91325
818-343-5762 Fax: 818-343-2041

Paul Haigh, AIA
Haigh . Architects . Designers
125 Greenwich Avenue
Greenwich, CT 06830
203-869-5445 Fax: 203-869-5033

Hanns Kainz & Associates
1099 Folsom Street
San Francisco, CA 94103
415-552-2600 Fax: 415-552-2602

Richard Hannum, AIA
Hannum Associates
222 Sutter Street, Suite 400
San Francisco, CA 94108
415-543-8333 Fax: 415-434-8705

Harper Mackay Ltd.
33-37 Charterhouse Square
London, EC1M 6EA
United Kingdom
0171-600-5151 Fax: 0171-600-1092

Michael Hayden
Thinking Lightly Inc.
5076 Hall Road
Santa Rosa, CA 95401
707-546-0664 Fax: 707-546-0661

Hillman Di Bernardo & Associates, Inc.
118 East 25th Street
New York City, NY 10010
212-529-7800 Fax: 212-979-9108

Mark R. Hornberger, AIA
Hornberger + Worstell
170 Maiden Lane, Suite 170
San Francisco, CA 94108
415-391-1080 Fax: 415-986-6387

Horton Lees Lighting Design
1011 Kearny Street
San Francisco, CA 94133
415-986-2575 Fax: 415-986-2576

Susan Huey, LIT
Lighting Integration Technology, Inc.
10 Arkansas Street
San Francisco, CA 94107
415-863-0313 Fax: 415-863-3923

Yutaka Inaba
Lighting Planners Associates, Inc.
2-9-3 Minami Aoyama, Minato-ku
Tokyo, 107 Japan
81-3-3-3796-1811 Fax: 81-3-3796-1810

Chip Israel, IALD, IES
Lighting Design Alliance
1234 East Burnett Street
Long Beach, CA 90806-3510
310-989-3843 Fax: 310-989-3847

Iwasaki Electric
3-12-4 Shiba, Minato-ku
Tokyo, 105 Japan
03-3796-8443

Alicia Jackson, IES, DLF
Electronics Lighting & Design
530 W. Francisco, Boulevard
San Rafael, CA 94901
415-258-9996 Fax: 415-258-0708

Joe Kaplan Lighting Design
9023 Hopen Place
Los Angeles, CA 90069
310-652-4795 Fax: 310-652-4797

Kajima Corporation
6-5-30 Akasaka, Minato-ku
Tokyo, 107 Japan
81-3-5661-2244 Fax: 81-3-5661-2264

Masahide Kakudate
Lighting Planners Associates, Inc.
2-9-3 Minami Aoyama, Minato-ku
Tokyo, 107 Japan
81-3-3-3796-1811 Fax: 81-3-3796-1810

Kaplan McLaughlin Diaz
222 Vallejo Street
San Francisco, CA 94111
415-398-5191 Fax: 415-394-7158

Frank Kelly
Imero Fiorentino Associates
33 West 60th Street
New York, NY 10019
212-246-0600 Fax: 212-246-6408

Kenji Kitani
Kitani Design Associates, Inc.
City Pole 4-5, 4-Chome,
Awatimachi Chuo-ku
Osaka, 541 Japan
06-232-1641 Fax: 06-232-1642

Steven L. Klein
Standard Electric Supply Co.
222 N. Emmber Lane
Milwaukee, WI 53233
1-800-776-8222 / 414-272-8100
Fax: 414-272-8111

Candace M. Kling, IES, IALD
C.M. Kling & Associates
1514 King Street
Alexandria, VA 22314
703-684-6270

Virva Kokkonen
S. Leonard Auerbach & Associates, Inc.
1045 Sansome Street, #218
San Francisco, CA 94111
415-392-7528 Fax: 415-392-7530

Linda Kondo
Clifford Selbert Design Collaborative
2067 Massachusetts Avenue
Cambridge, MA 02140
617-497-6605 Fax: 617-661-5772

Theo Kondos, IALD
Theo Kondos Associates
13 West 36th Street
New York, NY 10018
212-736-5510 Fax: 212-594-6332

William C. Lam
Lam Partners Inc.
84 Sherman Street
Cambridge, MA 02140
617-354-4502 Fax: 617-497-5038

Robert J. Laughlin, IALD
Robert J. Laughlin & Associates
180 Park Avenue North
Winter Park, FL 32789
407-740-0160 Fax: 407-629-0411

Svend Erik Laursen
Svend Erik Laursen A/S
Christian X s Vej 106, 8260 Aarhus,
Viby J
Denmark
45-86-14-85-33

LD Yamagiwa Laboratory
Tokyo, Japan
03-5210-5820

Douglas Leigh
The Douglas Leigh Organization
435 East 52nd Street, Room 7B
New York, NY 10022
212-223-8040

Yann Leroy, DPLG
Brennan Beer Gorman Monk /
Architects
515 Madison Avenue
New York, NY 10022
212-888-7663 Fax: 212-935-3868

Lighting Design Partnership Ltd.
4 John's Place
Edinburgh, EH6 7EL Scotland
440-131-553-6633 Fax: 440-131-553-3457

John G.H. Lum
John G.H. Lum Architect
165 Downey Street
San Francisco, CA 94117
415-753-1136 Fax: 415-753-2233

David Malman
Architectural Lighting Design
370 Brannan Street
San Francisco, CA 94107
415-495-4085 Fax: 415-4495-4660

Paul Marantz, IALD
Fisher Marantz Renfro Stone
126 Fifth Avenue
New York, NY 10011
212-691-3020 Fax: 212-633-1644

Brendt Markee
744 N 35th Street
Seattle, WA 98103
206-634-1270

Kousaku Matsumoto
Kitani Design Associates, Inc.
City Pole 4-5, 4-Chome,
Awatimachi Chuo-ku
Osaka, 541 Japan
06-232-1641 Fax: 06-232-1642

Max Fordham & Partners
42/43 Gloucester Crescent
London, NW1 7PE
United Kingdom
0171-267-5161 Fax: 0171-482-0325

Donald L. Maxcy, ASID
Donald Maxcy Design Associates
The Union Icehouse
600 East Franklin Street
Monterey, CA 93940
408-649-6582 Fax: 408-649-0519

Hayden McKay
Hayden McKay Lighting Design
31 West 21st Street
New York, NY 10010
212-727-2245 Fax: 212-727-2253

Calab McKenzie
Theo Kondos Associates
13 West 36th Street
New York, NY 10018
212-736-5510   Fax: 212-594-6332

Kauro Mende
Lighting Planners Associates, Inc.
2-9-3 Minami Aoyama, Minato-ku
Tokyo, 107 Japan
81-3-3796-1811 Fax: 81-3-3796-1810

Jeff Miller
Bent Severin & Associates
(formerly Lightsource, Inc.)
1927 Post Alley
Seattle, WA 98101
206-728-5665

Naomi Miller, IALD, IESNA
Lighting Research Center,
School of Architecture,
Rensselaer Polytechnic Institute
Troy Street
New York, NY 12180-3590
518-276-8718   Fax: 518-276-4835

Joel Miraglio
Miraglio Architecture + Design
381 Orange Street
Oakland, CA 949610
510-891-9145   Fax: 510-891-9107

Hideto Mori
Lighting Planners Associates, Inc.
2-9-3 Minami Aoyama, Minato-ku
Tokyo, 107 Japan
81-3-3796-1811 Fax: 81-3-3796-1810

Pam Morris
Pam Morris Exciting Lighting
14 East Sir Francis Drake
Larkspur, CA 94939
415-925-0840   Fax: 415-925-1305

Motoko Ishii Lighting Design
Mil Design House, 5-4-11, Sendagaya,
Shibuya-ku
Tokyo, 151 Japan
81-3-3353-5311 Fax: 81-3-3353-5120

Charles Morris Mount
300 W 108 Street, 2C
New York, NY 10025
212-864-2937   Fax: 212-864-0558

Jordan Mozer
Jordan Mozer & Associates, Ltd.
228 W. Illinois
Chicago, IL 60610
312-661-0060   Fax: 312-661-0981

Lana M. Nathe, IES
Standard Electric Supply Co.
222 N. Emmber Lane
Milwaukee, WI 53233
1-800-776-8222 / 414-272-8100
Fax: 414-272-8111

Catherine Ng, IES
Light Source
1210 18th Street
San Francisco, CA 94107
415-626-1210   Fax: 415-626-1821

Peter O Toole, IEEE, ASHE
RTKL Associates Inc.
Commerce Place
One South Street
Baltimore, MD 21202
410-528-8600   Fax: 410-385-2455

Kiku Obata
Kiku Obata & Company
5585 Pershing Avenue, Suite 240
St. Louis, MO 63112
314-361-3110   Fax: 314-361-4716

Alan Ohashi
Ohashi Design Studio
5739 Presley Avenue
Oakland, CA 94618
510-652-8840   Fax: 510-652-8604

Joy Ohashi
Ohashi Design Studio
5739 Presley Avenue
Oakland, CA 94618
510-652-8840   Fax: 510-652-8604

Terry Ohm
Impact Lighting and Production
One Mississippi
San Francisco, CA 94107
415-252-1182   Fax: 415-552-3002

Terry Ohm
Ohm Productions
601 Minnesota, Studio 225
San Francisco, CA 94107
415-641-1161

Yukio Oka
Rise Lighting Design Office
1-10-16-903 Minami Senba, Chuo-ku
Osaka, 542 Japan
06-266-3773   Fax: 06-266-3774

Norwood Oliver
Norwood Oliver Design Associates, Inc.
65 Bleecker Street
New York, NY 10012
212-982-7050   Fax: 212-674-2302

Richard Osborn
Luminae Souter Lighting Design
1740 Army Street, Second Floor
San Francisco, CA 94124
415-285-2622   Fax: 415-285-5718

Robert Osten, Jr.
Lam Partners Inc.
84 Sherman Street
Cambridge, MA 02140
617-354-4502   Fax: 617-497-5038

Takae Oyoke, IALD, IESNA, ASID
Lumenworks
1121 Ranleigh Way, Suite 100
Piedmont, CA 94610
510-835-7600   Fax: 510-836-2724

Nick Pagliante
Gallegos Lighting Design
8132 Andasol Avenue
Northridge, CA 91325
818-343-5762   Fax: 818-343-2041

Jerome Fuentes Paredes
Pacific Custom Finishes
15 B Sumner Street
San Francisco, CA 94103
415-241-0501   Fax: 415-282-7012

Richard Lee Parker, AIA
1581 Masonic Avenue
San Francisco, CA 94117
415-731-7572   Fax: 415-731-1410

Patrick Quigley & Associates
2340 Plaza del Amo, Suite 125
Torrance, CA 90501
310-533-6064   Fax: 310-320-3482

Paul Draper & Associates
4106 Swiss Avenue
Dallas, TX 75204
214-824-8352   Fax: 214-824-0932

Graham Phoenix, IALD
Lighting Design
63 Gee Street
London, ECIV 3RS United Kingdom
0171-250-3200 Fax: 0171-250-0824

Cosimo Pizzulli
Pizzulli Associates, Inc.
718 Wilshire Boulevard
Santa Monica, CA 90401-1708
310-393-9572   Fax: 310-458-6156

Craig A. Roeder
Craig A. Roeder Associates, Inc.
3829 North Hall Street
Dallas, TX 75219
214-528-2300   Fax: 214-521-2300

Lewis Rosenberg, IES, DLF
Electronics Lighting & Design
530 W. Francisco Boulevard
San Rafael, CA 94901
415-258-9996   Fax: 415-258-0708

Mark Rudiger
S. Leonard Auerbach & Associates, Inc.
1045 Sansome Street, #218
San Francisco, CA 94111
415-392-7528   Fax: 415-392-7530

Nobuyoshi Sakai
4-22-2 Kagamiike, Chikusaku
Nagoya-shi
Ehime Japan

Duane Schuler, IALD, IES
Schuler & Shook, Inc.
123 3rd Street N., Suite 216
Minneapolis, MN 56401
612-339-5958   Fax: 612-337-5097

Clifford Selbert
Clifford Selbert Design Collaborative
2067 Massachusetts Avenue
Cambridge, MA 02140
617-497-6605   Fax: 617-661-5772

Ms. Kristina Selles
Wheel Gersztoff Shankar Selles Inc.
138 W. 25th Street, 12th Floor
New York, NY 10001
212-947-6411   Fax: 212-643-1053

George S. Sexton III, IALD, IES
George Sexton Associates
3222 N Street, N.W., 5th Floor
Washington, DC
202-337-1903   Fax: 202-337-0047

Robert Shook, IALD, IES
Schuler & Shook, Inc.
213 West Institute Place
Chicago, IL 60610
312-944-8230   Fax: 312-944-8297

Thomas J. Skradski, ASID, MIES
Lumenworks
1121 Ranleigh Way, Suite 100
Piedmont, CA 94610
510-835-7600   Fax: 510-836-2724

Christina Spann
Lightspann
5753 Landregan Street
Emeryville, CA 94608
510-601-8500

Gerry Stebnicki
Stebnicki Robertson and Associates Ltd.
403, 1240 Kensington Road, N.W.
Calgary, Alberta T2N 3P7 Canada
403-270-8833   Fax: 403-270-9358

David Story
David Story Design
5609 Corson Avenue S.
Seattle, WA 98108
206-764-9815

Shunji Tamai
Mints Design Co., Ltd.
3-7-3 Kamiohsaki Shinagawa-ku
Tokyo, 141 Japan
03-5421-0321   Fax: 03-5421-0322

Toshio Tamura
Azu Sekkei Koro
1105 Grandbuild Edobori
1-23-19 Edobori, Nishi-ku
Osaka, 550 Japan
06-446-1015   Fax: 06-446-0705

Gustin Tan
Brennan Beer Gorman Monk / Interiors
515 Madison Avenue
New York, NY 10022
212-888-7663   Fax: 212-935-3868

Christopher Thompson, IALD, IES
Studio Lux
116 West Denny Way
Seattle, WA 98119
206-284-3417

TL Yamagiwa Laboratory
4-15-7 Nishishinjuku, Shinjuku-ku
Tokyo Japan
03-5371-1640

TL Yamagiwa Laboratory
4-5-18 Higashinippori, Arakawa-ku
Tokyo, 116 Japan
03-3803-6859   Fax: 03-3891-8853

Laura Tredinnick, IES
Schuler & Shook, Inc.
123 Third Street N., Suite 216
Minneapolis, MN 55401
612-339-5958   Fax: 612-941-0894

TRO/The Ritchie Organization
80 Bridge Street
Newton, MA 02158
617-969-9400   Fax: 617-527-6753

Stom Ushidate, DDA, JCD
Stom Ushidate + Interspace Time
Dai-ni Orient Building
5-13-11 Ueno Taito-ku
Tokyo, 110 Japan
03-3836-7293   Fax: 03-3836-0622

Ushiospax
2-43-15 Tomigaya, Shibuya-ku
Tokyo, 151 Japan
03-5478-7411   Fax: 03-5478-7400

D.R. Waite
Crossey Engineering Ltd.
4141 Yonge Street, Suite 305
Toronto, Ontario M2P 2A8 Canada
416-221-3111   Fax: 416-221-4354

Watry Design Group
1500 Fashion Island Boulevard #200
San Mateo, CA 94404
415-349-1546   Fax: 415-349-1384

William Whistler, AIA
Brennan Beer Gorman Monk / Interiors
515 Madison Avenue
New York, NY 10022
212-888-7663   Fax: 212-935-3868

Randall Whitehead, IALD, ASID Affiliate
Light Source
1210 18th Street
San Francisco, CA 94107
415-626-1210   Fax: 415-626-1821

Deborah Witte
The Lighting Group
200 Pine Street
San Francisco, CA 94104
415-989-3446   Fax: 415-989-4056

Jack Young
JRY Lighting & Sign
3665 W. Diablo
Las Vegas, NV 89118
702-739-6789   Fax: 702-739-9618

John Renton Young
JRY Lighting & Sign
3665 W. Diablo
Las Vegas, NV 89118
702-739-6789   Fax: 702-739-9618

Paul Zaferiou
Lam Partners Inc.
84 Sherman Street
Cambridge, MA 02140
617-354-4502   Fax: 617-497-5038

Nicholas P. Zalany
Richard P. Jencen Associates
2850 Euclid Avenue
Cleveland, OH 44115
216-781-0131   Fax: 216-781-0134

Gerry Zekowski
Gerry Zekowski Lighting Consultants Inc.
8256 E. Prairie
Skokie, IL 60076
708-673-4949   Fax: 708-673-4972

p h o t o g r a p h e r s

Russell Abraham
Russell Abraham Photography
60 Federal Street, Suite 303
San Francisco, CA 94107
415-896-6400   Fax: 415-896-6402

Anthony P. Albarello
80 Blackwells Mills Road
Somerset, NJ 08873
908-873-0319   Fax: 908-873-6977

Dennis Anderson
Dennis Anderson Photography
48 Lucky Drive
Greenbrae, CA 941904
415-332-7428   Fax: 415-927-2659

Yoshihisa Araki
Atelier Fukumoto Company
301 Crest Shinsaibachi
4-12-9, Minanisemba, Chuo-ku
Osaka, 542 Japan
06-245-4680   Fax: 06-245-4682

Jaime Ardiles-Arce
463 Fifth Avenue
New York, NY 10022
212-371-4749

Thomas Arledge
Arledge Studios
11616 Regency Drive
Potomac, MD 20854
301-983-5226

Chris Arthur
Transworld Eye
64 Gloucester Road
Kingston-Upon-Thames, KTI 3RB
United Kingdom
44-0181-546-4066

Fashid Assassi
Assassi Productions
P.O. Box 3651
Santa Barbara, CA 93130
805-682-2158   Fax: 805-682-1185

Yoshiteru Baba
Nacasa & Partners Inc.
3-5-5 Minami Azabu, Minato-ku
Tokyo, 106 Japan
03-3444-2922

Nash Baker
2208 Colquitt
Houston, TX 77098
713-529-5698

Richard Barnes
John Barnes Photography
1403 Shotwell
San Francisco, CA 94110
415-550-1023   Fax: 415-550-1023

Batista Moon Studio
10 Cillo Vista Drive
Monterey, CA 93940
408-373-1947   Fax: 408-373-5409

Alex Beatty
32 Lincoln Avenue
Lynnfield, MA 01940
617-334-4069

Mark Boisclair
Mark Boisclair Photography, Inc.
2400 East Thomas Road
Phoenix, AZ 85017
602-957-6997

Bresson Studio
2-9-16 Futabanosato, Higashi-ku
Hiroshima Japan
81-082-262-5500

Doug Brown
P.O. Box 2205
Alexandria, VA 22301
703-684-8778   Fax: 703-820-5589

Michael Bruk
Michael Bruk Photo / Graphics
731 Florida Street, #201
San Francisco, CA 94110
415-824-8600   Fax: 415-824-8375

Robert Burley
Design Archive
276 Carlaw Avenue, Suite 219
Toronto, Ontario M4M 2L1 Canada
416-466-0211   Fax: 416-465-2592

Steve Burns
Burns & Associates Inc.
2700 Sutter Street
San Francisco, CA 94115
415-567-4404   Fax: 415-567-4405

Tom Burt
Resort and Great Hotels
123 West Padre Street
Santa Barbara, CA 93105
805-687-1422   Fax: 805-682-8634

Dave Chawla
Chawla Associates
P.O. Box 26931
Las Vegas, NV 89126
702-253-6306

Langdon Clay
2221 Peachtree Road N.E.
Suite D-195
Atlanta, GA 30309
404-916-7265   Fax: 404-350-8004

David Clifton
David Clifton Photography
2637 W. Winnemec Street
Chicago, IL 60625
312-334-4346   Fax: 312-275-4175

Beatriz Coll
Coll Photography
2415 3rd Street
San Francisco, CA 94107
415-863-0699

Robt. Ames Cook
809 Hickory Highland Drive
Antioch, TN 37013
615-731-8855

Charles Cormany
845 5th Avenue
San Rafael, CA 94901
415-455-8784

George Cott
Chroma Inc.
2802 Azeele Street
Tampa, FL 33609
813-873-1374   Fax: 813-871-3448

Grey Crawford
1714 Lyndon Street
South Pasadena, CA 91030
213-413-4299

Cutter/Smith Photo Inc.
1645 E. Missouri
Phoenix, AZ 85016
602-274-5604   Fax: 602-265-0779

Dan Danilowicz
8882 Grandville
Detroit, MI 48228
313-273-1622

Mark Darley
311 Seymour Lane
Mill Valley, CA 94941
415-381-5452

Richard Davies
10 Steele s Road
London, NW3
England
0171-722-3032

Don Dubroff Photography
101 S. Catherine
LaGrange, IL 60525
708-482-0945

Engelhardt and Sellin
Postfach 120, 8000 Munchen 65
Germany
49-89-811-3903 Fax: 49-89-811-4610

Martin Fine
10072 Larwin Avenue #1
Chatsworth, CA 91322
818-341-7113

Dan Forer
Forer, Inc.
1970 N.E. 149th Street
North Miami, FL 33181
305-949-3131   Fax: 305-949-3701

Atelier Fukumoto
4-12-9-301 Minami Senba, Chuo-ku
Osaka Japan
81-06-245-4680 Fax: 81-06-245-4682

Masaaki Fukumoto
Atelier Fukumoto Company
301 Crest Shinsaibachi
12-9, 4-Chome Minanisemba, Chuo-ku
Osaka, 542 Japan
06-245-4680   Fax: 06-245-4682

Andrew Garn
Andrew Garn Photography
85 E. 10th Street
New York, NY 10003
212-353-8434

Dennis Gilbert
11 Furmage Street
London, SW18 4DF United Kingdom
0181-870-9051

Jeff Goldberg
Esto Photographics
222 Valley Place
Mamaroneck, NY 10543
914-698-4060

Anton Grassl
5 Sycamore Street
Cambridge, MA
617-876-1321

Mike Grosswendt
Michael Grosswendt Studio
5699 Kanan Road, #308
Agoura Hills, CA 91301
805-379-2489

Mark Gubin
K & S Photographies
250 Northwest Street
Milwaukee, WI 53202
414-271-6004   Fax: 414-271-8731

Ron Haisfield
1267 Battery Avenue
Baltimore, MD 21201

Steven Hall
Hedrich-Blessing
11 West Illinois Street
Chicago, IL 60610
312-321-1151

Lisa Carol Hardaway
Lisa Carol Hardaway & Paul Hester
Photography
P.O. Box 211
Fayetteville, TX 78940
408-378-4220

Mark F. Heffron
Mark F. Heffron Photography
P.O. Box 700
Milwaukee, WI 53201
414-962-0719

George Heinrich
1516 S. 7th Street
Minneapolis, MN 55454
612-338-2092

Paul Hester
Lisa Carol Hardaway & Paul Hester
Photography
P.O. Box 211
Fayetteville, TX 78940
408-378-4220

R. Greg Hursley
R. Greg Hursley, Inc.
4003 Cloudy Ridge Road
Austin, TX 78734
512-266-1391   Fax: 512-266-1392

Christopher Irion
183 Shipley Street
San Francisco, CA 94107
415-896-0752

Ben Janken
48 Agnon Avenue
San Francisco, CA 94112
415-206-1645   Fax: 415-648-1206

Alain Jaramillo
Blakeslee Group Inc.
916 N. Charles Street
Baltimore, MD 21218
410-727-8800

Toshio Kaneko
2-14 Minami Yamabushi-cho,
Shinjuku-ku
Tokyo, 162 Japan
03-3260-0992   Fax: 03-3260-2750

Elliot Kaufman
Elliot Kaufman Photography
255 W. 90th Street
New York, NY 10024
212-496-0860   Fax: 212-496-9104

Steve Keating
Steve Keating Photography
3411-A 33rd Avenue W.
Seattle, WA 98199
206-282-6456   Fax: 206-282-6506

Donna Kempner
P.O. Box 421190
San Francisco, CA 94142
415-771-1326
Fax: 415-474-0294

Klein & Wilson
7015 San Mateo Boulevard
Dallas, TX 75223
214-328-8627

Balthazar Korab
P.O. Box 895
Troy, MI 48099-0985
313-641-8881   Fax: 313-641-8889

Christian Korab
Balthazar Korab, Ltd.
2757 Emerson Avenue S.
Minneapolis, MN 55408
612-870-8947   Fax: 612-870-9034

Chris A. Little
P.O. Box 4067221
Atlanta, GA 30346
404-641-9688

Tim Long
Long Photography
Chicago, IL
312-718-5118

Marco Lorenzetti
c/o Hedrich-Blessing
11 West Illinois Street
Chicago, IL 60610
312-321-1151   Fax: 312-321-1165

Michael Lowry
2471 John Young Parkway
Orlando, FL 32804
407-291-1464

Maxwell MacKenzie
2641 Garfield Street, NW
Washington, DC 20008
202-232-6686

Jim Maguire
Maguire Photographics
875 Moe Drive
Akron, OH 44310
216-630-9070

Richard Mandelkorn
Richard Mandelkorn Photography
309 Waltham Street
Newton, MA 02165
617-332-3246   Fax: 617-332-3238

Akihisa Masuda
Motoko Ishii Lighting Design
Mil Design House, 5-4-11, Sendagaya,
Shibuya-ku
Tokyo, 151 Japan
81-3-3353-5311 Fax: 81-3-3353-5120

Yoshiharu Matsumura
14-13-201 Satsukigaoka Minama,
Suita-shi
Osaka Japan
81-06-330-3990 Fax: 81-06-330-1834

Matsushita Electric Works, Ltd.
1408 Kadoma
Kadoma, 571 Japan
06-908-6820

Terrance McCarthy
Terrance McCarthy Photography
3900 Del Mont Avenue
Oakland, CA 94605
510-430-9990

Scott McDonald
Hedrich-Blessing
11 W. Illinois Street
Chicago, IL 60610
312-321-1151

Norman McGarth
164 W. 79th Street
New York, NY 10024
212-799-6422   Fax: 212-799-1285

Chas McGrath
347 Corlano Court
Santa Rosa, CA 95404
707-824-8056   Fax: 707-824-8057

Max McKenzie
McKenzie Studio
2641 Garfield Street, N.W.
Washington, DC 20008
202-232-6686   Fax: 202-232-6684

Steve McLelland
4490 Dick Street
San Diego, CA 91789
909-598-7700   Fax: 909-598-3907

Nick Merrick
c/o Hedrich Blessing
11 West Illinois Street
Chicago, IL 60610
312-321-1151   Fax: 312-321-1165

Robert Mikrut
Robert E. Mikrut Architectural
Photography
63 Clinton Street
Newport, RI 02840
401-846-2134

Jon Miller
c/o Hedrich-Blessing
11 West Illinois Street
Chicago, IL 60610
312-321-1151   Fax: 312-321-1165

Tracy Miller
Creative Exposure
12 Black Mallard Road
Fairport, NY 14450
716-425-7594

Helmut Mitter
Weintraubengasse 14/10 A-1020
Vienna Austria
01143-1-21-404-53

Ira Montgomery
315 South Central Expressway
Dallas, TX 75201
214-748-8760
Fax: 214-748-8812

Hideto Mori
Lighting Planners Associates, Inc.
2-9-3 Minami Aoyama, Minato-ku
Tokyo, 107 Japan
81-3-3796-1811 Fax: 81-3-3796-1810

Motoko Ishii Lighting Design
Mil Design House, 5-4-11, Sendagaya,
Shibuya-ku
Tokyo, 151 Japan
81-3-3353-5311 Fax: 81-3-3353-5120

Gregory Murphey
P.O. Box 191
Trasalgar, IN 46181
812-597-011   Fax: 812-597-0114

Nacasa & Partners Inc.
3-5-5 Minami Azabu, Minato-ku
Tokyo, 106 Japan
03-3444-2922

Kurt Norregaard, MAA
Storchsvej 4, 200 Frederiksberg
Denmark
45-31-87-90-98

Nick Pagliante
Gallegos Lighting Design
8132 Andasol Avenue
Northridge, CA 91325
818-343-5762   Fax: 818-343-2041

Peter Paige
Peter Paige Photography
269 Parkside Road
Harrington Park, NJ 07640
201-767-3150   Fax: 201-767-9263

J.D. Peterson
Fotowork
896 Steiner
San Francisco, CA 94117
415-563-5606

Robert Pisano
Robert Pisano Photography
7527 15th Avenue N.E.
Seattle, WA 98115
206-525-3500   Fax: 206-525-2234

Neil Rashba
Neil Rashba Photographer
1178 Neck Road
Ponte Vedra Beach, FL 32082
904-273-0388   Fax: 904-355-8148

Kenneth Rice
Kenneth Rice Photography
456 61st Street
Oakland, CA 94609
510-652-1752   Fax: 510-658-4355

Sharon Risedorph
Sharon Risedorph Photography
761 Clementina Street
San Francisco, CA 94103
415-431-5851

Brian Rose
Prentice & Chan, Ohlhausen
14 E. 4th Street
New York, NY 10012
212-420-8600   Fax: 212-420-9842

Douglas A. Salin
647 Joost Avenue
San Francisco, CA 94127
415-584-3322

Sally Painter
2209 N.E. Klickitat
Portland, OR 97212
503-287-0227

Masami Sato
201 Ishii Building 3, Katamachi,
Shinjuku-ku
Tokyo Japan

Yoshio Shiratori
ZOOM
505 5-3 Minamimotomachi, Shinjuku-ku
Tokyo, 160 Japan
03-3353-0442   Fax: 03-3353-0458

Ron Starr
4104 24th Street, #358
San Francisco, CA 94114
415-541-7732   Fax: 415-285-9518

Juliet Stelzman
2393 Mission Street #1
San Francisco, CA 94110
415-282-9319

David Story
David Story Lighting Design
5609 Corson Avenue S.
Seattle, WA 98108
206-764-9815

Sun International, Inc.
915 N.E. 125th Street
North Miami, FL 332161
305-891-2500   Fax: 305-891-2682

John Sutton
John Sutton Photography
8 Main Street
Point San Quentin, CA 94964
415-258-8100   Fax: 415-258-8167

Robert Swanson
Swanson Images
532 Lisbon Street
San Francisco, CA 94112
415-585-6567   Fax: 415-587-8998

John Vaughan
John Vaughan Photography
319 Arkansas Street
San Francisco, CA 94107
415-550-7898   Fax: 415-550-8024

Hector Jorge Verdecchia
Monroe 1737
Buenos Aires, 1737
Argentina
541-784-9574   Fax: 541-784-3907

Peter Vitale
208 E. 60th Street
New York, NY 10022
212-888-6409

Paul Warchol
Paul Warchol Photographer
133 Mulberry Street, Apt. #6 S.
New York, NY 10013
212-431-3461   Fax: 212-274-1953

Warren Jagger Photography
150 Chestnut Street
Providence, RI 02906
401-351-7366   Fax: 401-421-7567

Matthew Weinreb
16 Millfield Lane
London, N6 6JD
United Kingdom
0181-340-6690 Fax: 0181-341-0441

Alan Weintraub
Alan Weintraub Photography
2325 3rd Street
San Francisco, CA 94107
415-553-8191   Fax: 415-553-8192

David Whitcomb
RTKL Associates Inc.
Commerce Place, One South Street
Baltimore, MD 21202
410-528-8600   Fax: 410-385-2455

Greg Wutke
Greg Wutke Photography
512 Polk
Monterey, CA 93940
408-375-7131

Yamagiwa Corporation
1-11-5 Sotokanda Chiyodaku
Tokyo Japan
3-3258-4536   Fax: 3-3251-2438

Yamagiwa Corporation
4-5-18 Higashi Nippori Arakawaku
Tokyo Japan
3-3803-6877   Fax: 3-3803-6854

Yoichi Yamazaki
Motoko Ishii Lighting Design
Mil Design House, 5-4-11, Sendagaya,
Shibuya-ku
Tokyo, 151 Japan
81-3-3353-5311 Fax: 81-3-3353-5120

Toshi Yoshimi
Toshi Yoshimi Photography
4030 Camero Avenue
Los Angeles, CA 90027
213-660-9043